BRISTOL & BATH
UNLOCKED

by
Emily Kerr
and
Joshua Perry

illustrations by
Katherine Hardy

CENTRAL BRISTOL

OUTER BRISTOL

BATH

N. SOMERSET

AROUND

ACROSS

TOP FIVES

NOTES

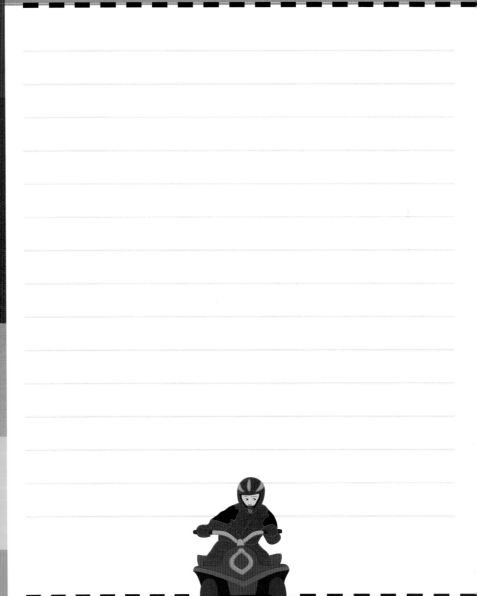

This book belongs to:

CENTRAL BRISTOL

OUTER BRISTOL

BATH

N. SOMERSET

AROUND

ACROSS

TOP FIVES

CONTENTS

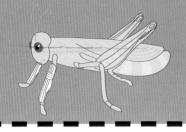

CENTRAL BRISTOL

OUTER BRISTOL

BATH

N. SOMERSET

AROUND

ACROSS

TOP FIVES

R I P

Tommy The Tractor

He will be wheely missed.

CENTRAL BRISTOL

OUTER BRISTOL

BATH

N. SOMERSET

AROUND

ACROSS

TOP FIVES

KEY

- Places
- Parks

CENTRAL BRISTOL

OUTER BRISTOL

BATH

N. SOMERSET

AROUND

ACROSS

TOP FIVES

GAZE INTO A GORGE

...on Clifton Suspension Bridge

Gazing into a gaping gorge may sound scary, but on this bridge it's perfectly safe. Stand on the pedestrian pavement and stare into the swirling river 76 metres below.

Clifton Suspension Bridge is a dramatic structure stretching across the Avon Gorge. It was designed by Isambard Kingdom Brunel when he was just 24 years old. Arguments about the design and a lack of money delayed the bridge's completion for 30 years. It was finally finished in 1864, five years after Brunel's death.

Sticker Scores

As you'll guess from the name, the bridge is 'suspended' above ground using massive chains, like a giant rope bridge. Trust us – it's safer than it sounds . . . and the view is *gorge*-ous!

5 SUSPENSION BRIDGE

4 STONE BRIDGE

3 RAILWAY BRIDGE

2 ROPE BRIDGE

1 GAME OF BRIDGE

CENTRAL BRISTOL

OUTER BRISTOL

BATH

N. SOMERSET

AROUND

ACROSS

TOP FIVES

Make A Day Of It

 Have a hot chocolate in Meme Chocolat, a café dedicated to the joys of everybody's favourite sweet treat. You'll find it on The Mall in nearby Clifton Village.

Visit a giant's cave and step inside a camera obscura at Clifton Observatory (see p18), which is right next to the bridge.

Photo Op
Stand at one end of the bridge and take a shot of you next to one of the massive chains that suspend it.

Fascinating Facts

⭐ **Before the bridge existed, there used to be an iron bar across the gorge. People brave enough would get in a basket and pay to be pulled across.**

⭐ People often propose marriage on the Clifton Suspension Bridge – but only if they aren't scared of heights!

⭐ **In 1885 a woman called Sarah Ann Henley tried to commit suicide by jumping from the bridge. However, she survived because her stiff Victorian skirt and petticoats acted as a parachute and slowed her fall!**

⭐ The chains that suspend the bridge are anchored twenty metres underground in the rocks at each end. That's as long as the length of a swimming pool! The chains have to be that deep or the bridge would collapse.

PLAN YOUR VISIT

Clifton Suspension Bridge
Clifton, BS8 4HA
www.cliftonbridge.org.uk

🕐 Bridge open 24 hours
Visitor Centre open daily 10.00-17.00

FREE (small charge for cars)

I want to go here ☐

← Clifton Suspension Bridge at night

SEEK OUT SINBAD THE SHIP'S CAT

...on the ss Great Britain

Cats are not well-known for their love of water, so a ship might seem a strange place to find one. However, in the old days ships often had lots of rats aboard, which ate the sailors' food. Cats were therefore kept as a cheap form of pest control.

The ss *Great Britain* is an enormous ship that used to carry passengers all over the world. It's now moored in Bristol, and you can look round and find out what life was like for people on board.

Pick up an audio tour when you arrive and use it to search for Sinbad the ship's cat, who was the crew's mascot. While you explore, sniff the ship's smells of fresh bread, engine oil and vomit (hopefully not your own!).

Sticker Scores

5 COOL CAT

4 BIG CAT

3 MEERKAT

2 PET CAT

1 CAT-ASTROPHE

CENTRAL BRISTOL

OUTER BRISTOL

BATH

N. SOMERSET

AROUND

ACROSS

TOP FIVES

Best Of The Rest

🔑 Check out the giant propeller beneath the boat that used to move the ship. And don't worry – these days the ship is docked on land so you won't drown while you're having a look!

🔑 Hunt for the talking toilet door. The ss *Great Britain* has the only speaking loo we've ever seen!

Top Tip

Once you've bought your ticket, you're allowed to come back again for free as many times as you like in a twelve month period.

← Kats: keep out!

Fascinating Facts

★ The ss *Great Britain* was launched in 1843, and at the time was by far the biggest boat in the world. She is exactly 98.15 metres long – that's the same length as 213 ship's cats (but less furry).

★ The ss *Great Britain* is another impressive construction designed by Isambard Kingdom Brunel. He was also responsible for the Clifton Suspension Bridge (see p10), the Great Western Railway (that ran from London to Exeter) and sliced bread. (OK, we made the last one up.)

Why did the ship find a husband so easily?

Because she was surrounded by buoys!

PLAN YOUR VISIT ②

Brunel's ss Great Britain
Great Western Dockyard, BS1 6TY
www.ssgreatbritain.org

📞 0117 926 0680

🕐 Daily (summer) 10.00-17.30
Daily (out of season) 10.00-16.30

££

I want to go here ☐

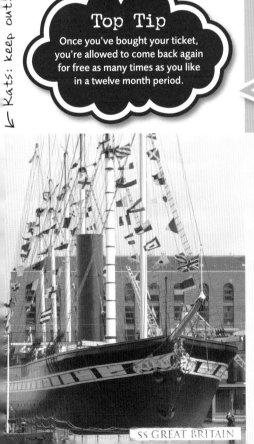

SS GREAT BRITAIN

MAKE YOUR OWN ANIMATIONS

...in At Bristol

Watching animations can be good fun, but making them is even better! If you fancy having a go, head over to At Bristol where you can create your very own 2D or 3D animation, email it home and even enter it into a competition. It's the biggest *draw* in town . . .

At Bristol is an interactive science centre in Bristol with the word 'at' in its name. ThAT's not something you see every day . . . and nor is their greAT selection of technology and animATion ATtractions!

The animation antics happen in the Animate It exhibition. You use the models and props to create your own moving masterpieces. Style your own characters, create a storyboard and then film a show reel. And don't worry if you get tired of this – there are over 300 other hands-on exhibits to explore!

Sticker Scores

5 CARTOON CHARACTER

4 PLASTICINE PERSON

3 ANIMATED ACTOR

2 SKETCHED STORY

1 SLOPPY SCRIBBLE

CENTRAL BRISTOL

OUTER BRISTOL

BATH

N. SOMERSET

AROUND

ACROSS

TOP FIVES

Best Of The Rest

 Visit the Planetarium – a huge dome lit up like the night sky! You'll discover coloured stars and giant planets, and learn how to navigate your way through space (which will be handy if you ever become an astronaut).

Zoom over to the flight zone. You can suspend a ball, launch a hot-air balloon or even create your own flying object! The time will just *fly* by.

← An amazing Attraction!

Photo Op

Take a picture of you standing in front of the giant silver ball (the Planetarium) that is outside At Bristol. See if you can get a snap of your face reflected in it!

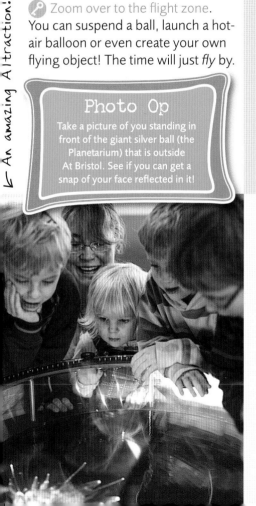

Fascinating Facts

★ **Bristol has a proud tradition of animation. It's the home town of Aardman Animations, who make the *Wallace and Gromit* films. Aardman also created a plasticine person called Morph who was popular in the 1970s and 1980s. Look out for him inside At Bristol's praxinoscope (an old animation machine).**

★ Children have 300 bones in their bodies whereas adults have only 206. But don't worry – you won't have joints extracted by a doctor when you become an adult. As you grow up, some of your bones will fuse together.

PLAN YOUR VISIT ③

At-Bristol
Anchor Road, Harbourside, BS1 5DB
www.at-bristol.org.uk

📞 **0845 345 1235**

🕐 **Mon-Fri (term time) 10.00-17.00
Sat-Sun, holidays 10.00-18.00**

£££

I want to go here ☐

STROKE A DINOSAUR

...at Bristol City Museum

If dinosaurs still roamed the earth, you wouldn't want to stroke one. You'd have a high chance of being either squished or eaten. Thankfully they became extinct 65 million years ago so you're unlikely to bump into one in the street . . .

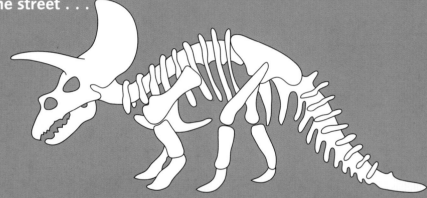

However, you can still stroke a dinosaur – sort of – at the Bristol City Museum. On display is a re-creation of a dinosaur's skin that you can run your hands along. The museum also has a good collection of real dinosaur fossils, which includes the most complete dinosaur skeleton ever found in Britain. It's called a Scelidosaur and it was a spiny, grass-eating dinosaur that lived around 200 million years ago. That makes it 199,999,089 years more ancient than an eleven year old!

Sticker Scores

5 — MAMMOTH MEGALOSAURUS

4 — VICIOUS VELOCIRAPTOR

3 — IRRITATED IGUANODON

2 — DYING DIPLODOCUS

1 — EXTINCT EUOPLOCEPHALUS

Best Of The Rest

🔑 Explore the history of Egypt. You'll find bits and bobs from tombs and burial sites, including some mummies. (We don't mean female parents, by the way.)

🔑 See precious stones in the rock gallery (as well as a few not-so-precious ones). Don't miss the stones which give out a strange purple glow under an ultraviolet light!

Top Tip
Pick up one of the kids' guides to the museum just inside the door at the information stand. It will help you to find your way around all the fun stuff.

Fascinating Facts

⭐ **The heaviest dinosaur was the brachiosaurus – an adult weighed up to 80 tonnes! That's as heavy as 88,888 kittens (but less suitable as a pet).**

⭐ The quetzalcoatlus didn't just have an unpronounceable name. It was also probably the largest flying creature of all time with a wingspan of up to thirteen metres! That's the same as 26 pigeons with their wings stretched tip to tip.

⭐ **The dinosaur with the longest name was the micropachycephalosaurus. This means tiny, thick-headed lizard. We think it should be called the hardtospellosaurus.**

Camarasaurus

Bristol City Museum and Art Gallery
Queen's Road, BS8 1RL
www.bristol.gov.uk/museums

📞 0117 922 3571
🕐 Daily 10.30-17.00

FREE 🍴 🎁 ☂

I want to go here ☐

CENTRAL BRISTOL

OUTER BRISTOL

BATH

N. SOMERSET

AROUND

ACROSS

TOP FIVES

Bigger than your average leg

GO INTO A GIANT'S CAVE

...at Clifton Observatory

If we were oversized people we wouldn't want to live in the Giant's Cave. The tunnel that leads to it is quite cramped, and there's not much space when you're inside either. However, it is a brilliant place for normal-sized people to get an amazing view!

The Giant's Cave sits halfway up the limestone cliffs of the Avon Gorge. Originally you had to climb the cliffs to get to it but nowadays there's a man-made tunnel which leads from the observatory at the top of the gorge down to a balcony within the cave. Look through the metal bars and you'll be able to see into the gorge over 70 metres below. It's a remarkable sight at a great height!

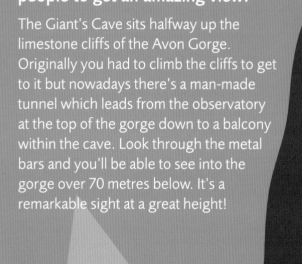

Sticker Scores

5 — CAVE

4 — DUNGEON

3 — CAVERN

2 — GROTTO

1 — GROTTY

CENTRAL BRISTOL

OUTER BRISTOL

BATH

N. SOMERSET

AROUND

ACROSS

TOP FIVES

Best Of The Rest

🔑 Spy on passers-by in the Clifton Observatory's Camera Obscura. You'll see live pictures of the outside world beamed onto the table in front of you without any electronic equipment!

🔑 Gawp at the Giant's Cave from the Clifton Suspension Bridge (see p10).

Photo Op

Stand on the cave's balcony and take a snap of the gorge below. Just be careful not to fall over the edge!

← Yazing out from a giant's cave

Fascinating Facts

⭐ **The giants that gave their names to the cave were called Goram and Vincent. According to local legend, these two brothers fought over a woman called Avona. This might explain why the river below the cave is called the Avon . . . but then again it could all just be a *tall* tale!**

⭐ The tunnel that leads from the observatory to the Giant's Cave was opened in 1837 and is 610 metres long. That's the same length as 410 eleven year olds lying end to end!

⭐ **It is thought that 1,700 years ago the cave was joined to an ancient chapel. At some point the chapel detached from the cliff and crumbled into the gorge beneath. We hope no one was in there at the time!**

PLAN YOUR VISIT 5

Clifton Observatory and the Giant's Cave

Clifton Down, BS8 3LT

📞 0117 974 1242

🕐 Daily (summer) 10.30-17.00
Weekends (out of season) 10.30-16.00

£

I want to go here ☐

FEED THE LORIKEETS

...at Bristol Zoo

If you've never seen a lorikeet before, then you're in for a surprise as it's the brightest bird imaginable. It looks like someone's taken a new set of felt-tip pens and used them to colour in the feathers!

At Bristol Zoo you not only get to admire these lovely rainbow-coloured birds – you can also feed them pots of nectar by hand! It's a sweet treat for a lorikeet . . .

Of course, there's plenty more to do while you're at the zoo. You can stroll along underwater walkways to see the seals and penguins or head to the Zoolympics trail where you can run, jump and measure yourself against some of the most impressive animals in the world.

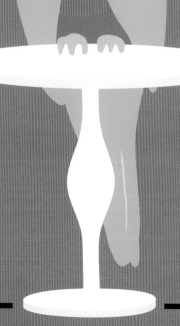

Sticker Scores

5	4	3
LOVEABLE LORIKEET	CUTE CANARY	PLEASANT PARROT

2	1
MOUTHY MACAW	PUDGY BUDGIE

Best Of The Rest

🔑 Swing through the trees on ZooRopia. This aerial assault course is right in the centre of the zoo and themed around tree-dwelling animals. You get strapped to a safety harness . . . then off you go!

🔑 Hold bugs at an Animal Encounters session in the Terrace Theatre. Don't miss the Madagascan hissing cockroach!

🔑 Rock up to the Reptile House where you can see reptiles (like snakes and crocodiles) and amphibians (like frogs and turtles).

← A meerkat (not a lorikeet!)

Fascinating Facts

⭐ The Reptile House's largest inhabitant is Biggie, the giant tortoise. He weighs over 175 kilogrammes, which is as heavy as four ten year olds.

Top Tip
If you're planning to visit in summer, check out the zoo's music and theatre events. They host open-air plays, concerts, and a family festival in July.

What do you call a snake on the front of your car?
A windscreen viper!

PLAN YOUR VISIT ⑥

Bristol Zoo
Clifton, BS8 3HA
www.bristolzoo.org.uk

📞 0117 974 7300

🕐 Daily (summer) 09.00-17.30
Daily (out of season) 09.00-17.00

£££

I want to go here ☐

CENTRAL BRISTOL
OUTER BRISTOL
BATH
N. SOMERSET
AROUND
ACROSS
TOP FIVES

SLIDE DOWN A ROCK

...on the Clifton Rock Slide

Most slides are made of plastic or metal. That's because plastic and metal are nice and slippery. Rock, on the other hand, is usually, well . . . rocky. However, this particular rock has been worn so smooth you can actually slide down it!

Close to the Clifton Suspension Bridge (see p10) is an open limestone rock face with a slide running through the middle of it. Generations of kids (and quite a few adults) have zoomed down this rock, and each person's sliding bottom has helped to polish the stone into a slippery surface. It may not be quite as smooth as a normal slide, but where else do you get to slide on stone? In any case, we think it *rocks*!

Sticker Scores

5	4	3
ROCK FACE	LOG FLUME	WATER CHUTE

2	1
SIMPLE SLIDE	BANANA SKIN

CENTRAL BRISTOL

OUTER BRISTOL

BATH

N. SOMERSET

AROUND

ACROSS

TOP FIVES

Wheeeeee! ⌐

Fascinating Facts

★ People have lived close to the slide for thousands of years. Nearby Clifton Down is home to the remnants of an Iron Age hill fort. A Roman road also ran through the area. So it's possible that Roman bums helped to smooth the surface of the Clifton rock slide!

★ Limestone is used for plenty of things apart from sliding. It's an ingredient in cement, glass and even toothpaste.

What is a stone's favourite music?
Rock 'n' roll!

Top Tip

The slide's at its best when it's dry, so make sure you go there on a sunny day. Wear soft trousers, such as tracksuit bottoms (jeans aren't very good), or just sit on a jumper instead.

Photo Op

Get a snap as you're sliding down the rock. Hold your arms in the air and shout 'Rock slide!' as you whizz along!

PLAN YOUR VISIT ⑦

Clifton Rock Slide

Clifton Down, Nr Clifton Suspension Bridge

FREE

I want to go here ☐

DANCE ON ICE
...at Bristol Ice Rink

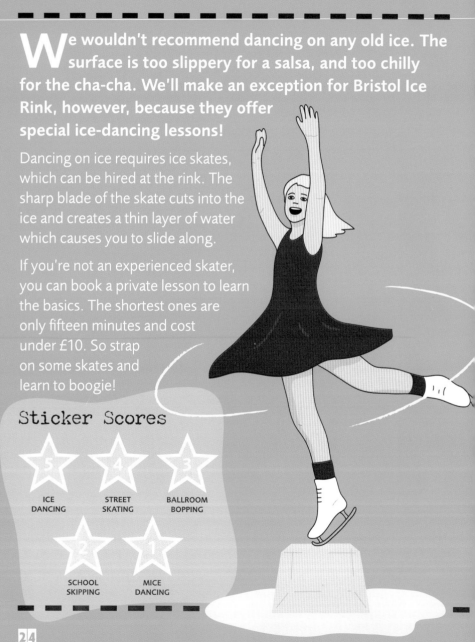

We wouldn't recommend dancing on any old ice. The surface is too slippery for a salsa, and too chilly for the cha-cha. We'll make an exception for Bristol Ice Rink, however, because they offer special ice-dancing lessons!

Dancing on ice requires ice skates, which can be hired at the rink. The sharp blade of the skate cuts into the ice and creates a thin layer of water which causes you to slide along.

If you're not an experienced skater, you can book a private lesson to learn the basics. The shortest ones are only fifteen minutes and cost under £10. So strap on some skates and learn to boogie!

Sticker Scores

5	4	3
ICE DANCING	STREET SKATING	BALLROOM BOPPING
2	1	
SCHOOL SKIPPING	MICE DANCING	

CENTRAL BRISTOL

OUTER BRISTOL

BATH

N. SOMERSET

AROUND

ACROSS

TOP FIVES

← Not dancing on ice!

Photo Op

Take a snap of you smiling as you whizz around the rink. If you can't whizz, just take a snap of you smiling and holding onto the rails!

Fascinating Facts

⭐ **The most famous British ice dancers are Jayne Torvill and Christopher Dean. This creative couple won an ice-dancing gold medal at the 1984 Winter Olympics. The judges all scored them with a perfect 6.0 for the free dance. That means their routine was flawless (but not floor-less – they still needed ground underneath them!).**

⭐ Creating an ice rink involves more than just chucking some water onto a cold surface. It's a complicated process that involves putting down ten to fifteen thin layers of water and freezing them one at a time. When coloured markings are required (such as for ice hockey), the paint is added to the second or third layer.

 PLAN YOUR VISIT **8**

Bristol Ice Rink

Frogmore Street, BS1 5NA

www.jnlbristol.co.uk

📞 0117 929 2148

🕐 Times vary – check online
Public sessions often 10.00-15.00
and 16.30-18.00

£££

I want to go here ☐

FLOAT ON A BOAT

...around Bristol Harbour

Bristol is built on the junction of two rivers, so one of the best ways to see it is from the water. However, we're not suggesting you swim through the city – just take a ferry around the harbour to see the dockside sights!

The yellow and blue boats of the Bristol Ferry Boat Company run through the heart of Bristol. Along the way you'll see the ss *Great Britain* (see p12) and the *Matthew* (a replica of an old wooden boat). You'll also see several big, red warehouses which used to store tobacco, and the Underfall Boatyard where boats are still built today. All in all it's a *ferry* nice way to spend a day!

Sticker Scores

5 — FANTASTIC FERRY

4 — SUPER SHIP

3 — DECENT DINGHY

2 — RUBBISH ROWING BOAT

1 — MAN OVERBOARD!

CENTRAL BRISTOL

OUTER BRISTOL

BATH

N. SOMERSET

AROUND

ACROSS

TOP FIVES

Top Tip

The company runs several themed rides. These include a Sail with Santa cruise at Christmas, plus cream tea, wildlife and poetry trips during the rest of the year.

Photo Op

Take a picture of yourself sailing on the ferry, with one of Bristol's distinctive red warehouses behind you.

Why can't you sail in a bathroom basin?

Because it would sink!

← Floating through Bristol on a ferry

Fascinating Facts

★ Bristol harbour has a shameful secret. Hundreds of years ago these docks were part of the slave trade, which involved buying people in Africa then transporting them to work in the West Indies in terrible conditions without being paid.

★ Another big Bristol business was tobacco, which was often traded in exchange for slaves. Many of the warehouses you will see beside the docks were built as part of this horrific industry.

★ The largest ferry in the world runs between England and Ireland. It's got enough space to fit 2,000 passengers, 1,300 cars and 260 lorries or coaches. The largest *fairy* in the world, on the other hand, is much harder to measure, since we're not even sure that fairies exist!

PLAN YOUR VISIT 9

Bristol Ferry Boat Company

Welsh Back, BS1 4SP
(Company office – check website for departure points)
www.bristolferry.com

📞 0117 927 3416

🕐 Daily 07.30-18.00
(frequency varies by route and season)

£

I want to go here ☐

SEE MODERN ART

...at Arnolfini

We don't include many art galleries in our books. That's because most seem to be filled with paintings of flowers and naked women. *Yawn!* Modern art is different though – you just never know what you're going to get!

Arnolfini is a big contemporary arts centre. That's a fancy way of saying they have loads of cultural things going on there, like cinema and dance and storytelling. However, we particularly like the modern-art exhibitions because they're so random. Past examples have included an exhibition of things beginning with the letter C, and a Supertoys season where visitors could play with, destroy or re-make toys! Now that's our kind of gallery . . .

Sticker Scores

5 MODERN ART	4 COOL CINEMA	3 SUPER STORYTELLING
2 DECENT DANCE	1 FLOWER PAINTING	

CENTRAL BRISTOL

OUTER BRISTOL

BATH

N. SOMERSET

AROUND

ACROSS

TOP FIVES

Best Of The Rest

Watch boats go by from the terrace outside the centre. Arnolfini is beside the Bristol Docks, so it's a perfect place to sit in the sun and watch the river.

Top Tip

Every few months Arnolfini runs Mash Up events for kids on Saturday afternoons. They're inspired by current exhibitions, and you could find yourself having a go at drawing, painting, video making or storytelling. Check the website for details.

QUICK ON THE DRAW ...

Fascinating Facts

⭐ Modern art is sometimes so unusual that nobody really knows what it's supposed to look like. A picture called The Boat was hung upside down for two months in New York's Museum of Modern Art during 1961. None of the 116,000 visitors noticed!

⭐ The largest statue of a horse in the world is the Zizkov Monument in Prague, which is nine metres tall. That's higher than five actual horses standing on top of each other (though less likely to fall over).

Photo Op

Copy the pose of the sitting man sculpture outside Arnolfini. Perch on the spare bit of statue, lean your hands on your knees and assume a serious expression!

PLAN YOUR VISIT 10

Arnolfini

16 Narrow Quay, BS1 4QA

www.arnolfini.org.uk

📞 0117 917 2300

🕐 Tue-Sun & bank holidays 11.00-18.00

FREE

I want to go here ☐

RIDE THE HARBOURSIDE STEAM TRAIN

...on the Bristol Harbour Railway

If you needed to travel speedily between two places, the chances are you wouldn't choose an old train. However, if you want a scenic view of Bristol Harbour there aren't many better options than the dockside steam train!

The Bristol Harbour Railway was once used for transporting goods around the port but nowadays it's a tourist route running on select summer days. The steam engines which pull the train are more than 70 years old and are still going strong!

You board the train by the ss *Great Britain* (see p12) and travel through some of the best bits of the docks. Check out the funky cranes by the old industrial museum as you chug past. Full steam ahead!

Sticker Scores

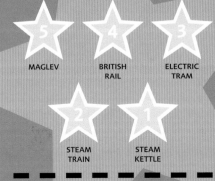

5 — MAGLEV

4 — BRITISH RAIL

3 — ELECTRIC TRAM

2 — STEAM TRAIN

1 — STEAM KETTLE

Similar Spots

🔑 The docks aren't the only place you can ride on a mini train near Bristol. Check out these enter-*train*-ing rides . . .

Ashton Court Miniature Steam Railway (see p42). You sit astride a mini carriage while a steam or diesel train takes you along a small set of tracks. Summer Sundays only.

Avon Valley Railway Nr Keynsham. This local steam railway is five miles long. They hold regular events, including days with Thomas the Tank Engine. And if you're a real train spotter, you can even have your birthday on board!

← Choo choo!

Fascinating Facts

⭐ **The fastest train in the world is in Shanghai, China. It's called the MagLev (because it *Mag*netically *Lev*itates) and reaches speeds of up to 268 mph!**

⭐ The world's biggest model train set is based in a warehouse in Germany. It will have almost 13 miles of track when it's finished in 2014. That's around thirteen times as long as Bristol's dockside railway.

Top Tip
Get a bacon butty from Brunel's Buttery just along the harbour to keep you going during your journey. It's a Bristol institution and well worth a visit!

Which locomotive is made of caramel?
A *chew-chew* train!

PLAN YOUR VISIT 11

Bristol Harbour Railway
Departs next to ss Great Britain (see p12)
www.bristol.gov.uk
📞 0117 9223571
🕐 Weekends (summer) 11.00-17.00
£

I want to go here ☐

OUTER BRISTOL

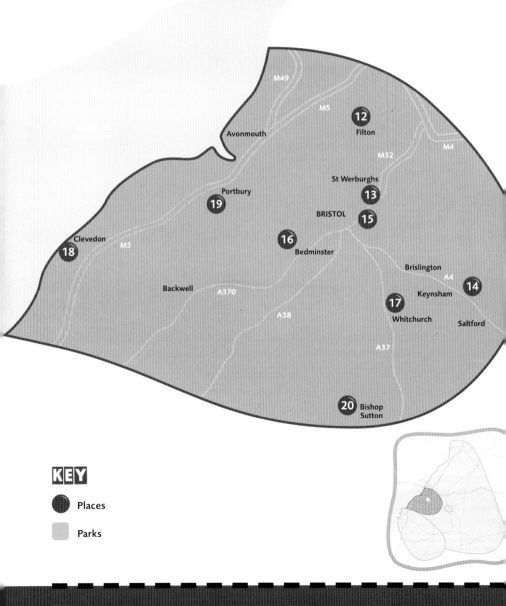

KEY

🔴 Places

🟦 Parks

CENTRAL BRISTOL

OUTER BRISTOL

BATH

N. SOMERSET

AROUND

ACROSS

TOP FIVES

KONCORDE

WAVERLEY

CLIMB INTO A CONCORDE

...at Concorde at Filton

Until 2003 Concorde was the fastest passenger plane on earth. Now it's the slowest, achieving exactly 0 mph! That's because sadly these supersonic aircraft no longer fly – but it's still great fun to see one.

Concorde 216 was the last one ever made. Now that all Concordes have retired, 216 spends its time in Filton, which was one of two sites where they were built. In total, Concorde 216 spent 18,257 hours flying – that's the equivalent of two years in the air!

KONCORDE

Sticker Scores

5	4	3
CONCORDE	JUMBO JET	PROPELLER PLANE
2	1	
GLIDER	GROUNDED	

Concorde at Filton offers great guided tours of the supersonic plane. You get to see the hangar where Concordes used to be built, and actually step inside the aircraft. It makes other forms of transport look *plane* boring!

CENTRAL BRISTOL

OUTER BRISTOL

BATH

N. SOMERSET

AROUND

ACROSS

TOP FIVES

Similar Spots

 If you enjoy seeing a Concorde close up, check out the Fleet Air Arm Museum (see p72). It's got a whole load of fascinating aeroplanes as well as its own Concorde.

Top Tip

For safety reasons, children under five are not allowed to visit Concorde. (Maybe it's to stop them accidentally pressing the 'Takeoff' button!)

Photo Op

Stand beside the plane and hold your arms out behind you like the wings of a Concorde.

Fascinating Facts

★ Concorde was a joint project between the British and French governments and got its name from the French word for agreement. Presumably people were so amazed that the two countries had managed to work together that this fact was worth celebrating!

★ Concorde first flew in 1969, and at the time was the world's only supersonic passenger aircraft. Supersonic means something that travels faster than the speed of sound, which is 768 mph. That's 25,000 times faster than a snail!

★ The record flight time for Concorde between London and New York was under three hours! A regular jumbo jet would take six hours to fly the same distance.

PLAN YOUR VISIT 12

Airbus Factory

Filton, BS34 7QS
Parking arrangements vary – check website
www.concordeatfilton.org.uk

 0117 936 5485

 Wed-Sun: tours at 10.00, 12.00 & 14.00
Advance booking required

££

I want to go here ☐

BOTTLE-FEED BABY GOATS

...at St Werburghs City Farm

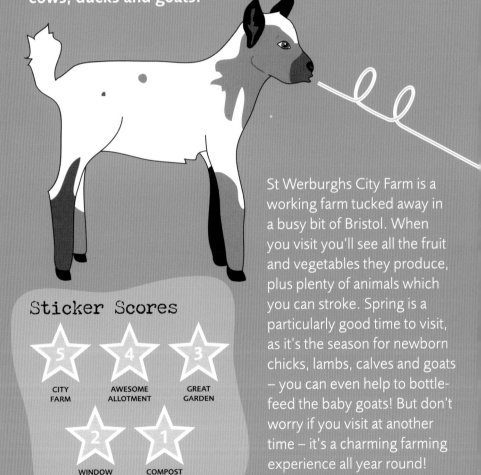

Cities are usually full of things like shopping centres and traffic jams. So it comes as quite a surprise to find that Bristol contains a real farm, complete with pigs, cows, ducks and goats!

Sticker Scores

5 — CITY FARM

4 — AWESOME ALLOTMENT

3 — GREAT GARDEN

2 — WINDOW BOX

1 — COMPOST HEAP

St Werburghs City Farm is a working farm tucked away in a busy bit of Bristol. When you visit you'll see all the fruit and vegetables they produce, plus plenty of animals which you can stroke. Spring is a particularly good time to visit, as it's the season for newborn chicks, lambs, calves and goats – you can even help to bottle-feed the baby goats! But don't worry if you visit at another time – it's a charming farming experience all year round!

Best Of The Rest

 Scramble around the adventure playground within the grounds of the farm. There are plenty of things to clamber over, climb up or slide down.

 Snack at the on-site organic café, which uses eggs, meat and vegetables from the farm. It also runs cool cookery classes.

 Climb in a converted church. Nearby St Werburghs church has been converted into an awesome climbing centre. Check out their weekly Rockhoppers club for kids aged seven to ten. www.undercover-rock.com

Similar Spots

 Windmill Hill City Farm in Bedminster is another working farm, with pigs, ducks, chickens and more. www.windmillhillcityfarm.org.uk

Top Tip

During the summer, St Werburghs runs one-week camps. You explore the farm, make dens, follow nature trails and meet lots of animals.

What does a cow do for entertainment? *Bull*-room dancing!

PLAN YOUR VISIT 13

St Werburghs City Farm
Watercress Rd, St Werburghs, BS2 9YJ
www.swcityfarm.org.uk

📞 0117 942 8241

🕐 Daily (summer) 09.00-17.00
Daily (out of season) 09.00-16.00

FREE 🍴

I want to go here ☐

CENTRAL BRISTOL

OUTER BRISTOL

BATH

N. SOMERSET

AROUND

ACROSS

TOP FIVES

GO WILD

...at Avon Valley Adventure Park

It's hard to describe Avon Valley Park because there's just so much to do there. It's got everything from animals to fairground rides. Just don't try it all at once or you might end up on the dodgems with a donkey!

The park has something for everyone. If animals are your thing, you can see shire horses and pot-bellied pigs, or cuddle cute things in the pets' corner.

Sticker Scores

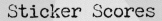

5	4	3
SUMMER HOLIDAYS	WEEKEND	AFTER SCHOOL

2	1
PLAYTIME	NAUGHTY STEP

Alternatively, if you're more into machines, you can chug round a mini railway, or hop on a tractor train and be pulled across the fields. If you like excitement you can also try out a pedal go-kart or a quad bike. We guarantee you'll have a lark in this park!

CENTRAL BRISTOL

OUTER BRISTOL

BATH

N. SOMERSET

AROUND

ACROSS

TOP FIVES

Best Of The Rest

 Watch a falconry display. You'll see peregrine falcons, barn owls and several other breeds of birds.

 Challenge yourself on the junior assault course. You get to scramble over logs and under nets along this riverside track.

 Go boating on the lake. It can be quite hard work, so take a strong grown-up with you!

Top Tip

Opening hours and show times vary by attraction and by day, so do check online before you go if there's something you particularly want to visit!

Fascinating Facts

⭐ **Peregrine falcons are the fastest creatures on earth. They can dive at speeds of over 200 mph when they're trying to catch prey. So we advise you not to get in the way . . . unless you want to end up as falcon food!**

⭐ The shire is the biggest type of British horse. They have long white hairs (known as feathers) on their feet, and used to be used for heavy work like pulling along beer carts. Their name comes from the fact that the horses were originally from the 'shire counties, such as Lincolnshire and Cambridgeshire. It's not because they are *shy-er* than other animals!

What do you call someone who is squashed between two llamas?
Llama-nated!

PLAN YOUR VISIT 14

Avon Valley Adventure & Wildlife Park

Pixash Lane, Bath Road, Keynsham, BS31 1TP

www.avonvalleycountrypark.com

📞 **0117 986 4929**

🕐 **Daily (summer) 10.00-18.00**

££ 🍴 🎁 ❗

I want to go here ☐

CYCLE ALONG A DISUSED RAILWAY

...on the Bristol and Bath railway path

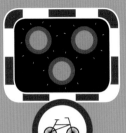

Normally we definitely wouldn't recommend cycling along a railway. First, you'd be likely to get squished, and second, the tracks would make it bumpy. However, in this case we're talking about a disused railway line that has been turned into a cycle path . . .

This thirteen-mile track runs from Bristol to Bath, starting at St Philip's Road in Bristol and ending at Pulteney Bridge in Bath. If you're feeling super-sporty you can also extend your journey by cycling along the Kennet and Avon canal path (see p64).

The railway has been covered in Tarmac so it's easy to cycle on. Look out for the cool sculptures and other artwork along the route. It's a *rail*-ly good way to get some exercise!

Sticker Scores

5 MOTORBIKE

4 MOUNTAIN BIKE

3 PENNY-FARTHING

2 UNICYCLE

1 ON YER BIKE

CENTRAL BRISTOL

OUTER BRISTOL

BATH

N. SOMERSET

AROUND

ACROSS

TOP FIVES

Similar Spots

Cycle from Bristol to Portishead along the Avon Gorge. You go under Clifton Suspension Bridge (see p10) then along an off-road track next to steep cliffs. Take a swimming costume and you could also pop to Portishead's open-air swimming pool when you arrive.

Top Tip

During the summer, take a picnic and stop for a snack beside one of the sculptures along the path. And if you're too tired to cycle home you can always return on one of the trains that run regularly between Bristol and Bath.

← Not all of the railway line is out of use!

Fascinating Facts

★ **The Tour de France is the world's best-known bike race. The course is a whopping 2,241 miles long – that's 170 times as long as the Bristol–Bath cycle track! Confusingly, while the race mostly takes place in France, the route often crosses other countries. In 2007 it actually started in London.**

★ The cycling world speed record is held by Bruce Bursford, who reached an astonishing 208 mph on his bike. That's about three times the UK motorway speed limit!

Why are bicycles always exhausted?
Because they are two-tyred!

PLAN YOUR VISIT 15

Bristol and Bath Railway Path
www.bristolbathrailwaypath.org.uk

☎ 0117 922 4325

FREE

I want to go here ☐

LEARN TO PLAY GOLF

...in Ashton Court

Golf clubs are often full of old men in blazers talking about bogeys. That may not sound like loads of fun, but Ashton Court is different. Its golf courses are open to all ages, whether or not you pick your nose!

Ashton Court is a pretty estate which is great for kite flying, bike riding and general running around. However, we particularly like the golf. Their two courses are great for beginners, and if you've never played before you can book a golf lesson for you and your family.

As for bogeys, this is the word golfers use to describe a bad score on a hole. It may sound funny to you, but to a golfer it's *snot*!

Sticker Scores

5	4	3
IN THE HOLE	ON THE GREEN	IN THE ROUGH

2	1
IN THE BUNKER	DOUBLE BOGEY

Best Of The Rest

🔑 Go off-road biking or grass skiing on Ashton Court's hills in the summer. Alternatively, try some tobogganing in the winter.

🔑 Check out the cool sculptures hidden around the grounds.

🔑 Ride the miniature railway which operates some weekends during the summer.

🔑 Spot some deer in the ancient deer park, which has been there since the 1300s.

← It's behind you!

Photo Op
Pose with your club poised to smash a golf ball! Or find the open door sculpture in the park and take a snap of you walking into it.

Fascinating Facts

★ Every year Ashton Court hosts some amazing festivals. There's the Balloon Fiesta in August, which shows off every imaginable shape and size of hot-air balloon and attracts around 150,000 visitors per day. Then there's the Kite Festival in September, where you can admire people's crazy flying contraptions (see p112).

Top Tip
If you're just starting to play golf, use a tee (a plastic ball holder) every time you hit a shot from off the green. You'll find it easier to make a clean connection.

PLAN YOUR VISIT 16
Ashton Court Estate
Long Ashton, BS41
(use Clifton Lodge entrance for golf course)
www.cliftoncollegeuk.com/ccsl/golf/

📞 0117 973 8508
🕐 Daily 07.00-18.30 (or dusk)
££

I want to go here ☐

GROOM A HORSE

...at Horseworld Animal Sanctuary

Horseworld is home to plenty of interesting creatures, from mini ponies to massive shire horses – it's obvious which animals are the *mane* attraction!

Horseworld is a charity that rescues abandoned or badly treated animals. As well as equine (horse-like) creatures they've also saved ferrets, goats, cockatiels and even a pot-bellied pig!

We particularly like their Touch and Groom sessions where you get to stroke and pet the horses. And best of all, part of the entry cost goes towards rescuing more animals. So just by visiting you're helping to make the world a happier place for horses!

Sticker Scores

5	4	3
STRAPPING SHIRE	TOWERING THOROUGHBRED	AVERAGE ARABIAN

2	1
SHAGGY SHETLAND	PUNY PONY

Best Of The Rest

 Visit the play barn, where you'll find an adventure playground, a seriously long slide and straw bales to clamber over and gallop around.

 See if you're as strong as a horse in the interactive centre. You and your friends can pull against a weight and see how many of you it takes to generate one horsepower!

Photo Op
Take a pic of you cuddling your favourite rescued animal. Just be careful not to use the flash – it can scare the animals.

← Hanging out with a horse

Fascinating Facts

★ **All thoroughbred horses in the world today are descended from three stallions and 74 mares. Every thoroughbred has paperwork tracing its full family tree!**

★ Camargue horses, from France, are born black but then turn completely white as they become adults.

★ **Horses are measured in hands. A hand is around ten centimetres long and, unsurprisingly, the measurement is based on the width of a human hand. If you want to measure a horse just count the number of hand widths from the ground to its shoulders – *hand-y!*

★ Any horse less than 14.2 hands high is called a pony.

What is the most fashionable horse in the world? A clothes horse!

PLAN YOUR VISIT 17

HorseWorld
Staunton Manor Farm, Staunton Lane, Whitchurch, BS14 0QJ

www.horseworld.org.uk

📞 **01275 540 173**

🕐 **Daily (summer) 10.00-17.00
Wed-Sun (out of season) 10.00-16.00**

£€

I want to go here ☐

CENTRAL BRISTOL
OUTER BRISTOL
BATH
N. SOMERSET
AROUND
ACROSS
TOP FIVES

TAKE A TRIP ON A PADDLE STEAMER

...on the Waverley

You can't buy much for a pound. It might get you one and a half chocolate bars, perhaps, or maybe a spoon. Oh, and it is also just enough to buy you a 693 tonne steamship!

The *Waverley* was bought by the Paddle Steamer Preservation Society – for the massive sum of a pound! However, it's not quite as much of a bargain as it sounds – the society has spent lots of money restoring her so she's fit for active service.

These days the *Waverley* sails all around the coast of the UK from Easter to autumn, and you can hop aboard for a cruise along the Bristol Channel. She's the last paddle steamer in the world still sailing and we think it was a pound well spent!

Sticker Scores

5 PADDLE STEAMER

4 STEAM ENGINE

3 STEAM ROOM

2 STEAM IRON

1 VEGETABLE STEAMER

~ "I thought you said 'Go right'!"

CENTRAL BRISTOL

OUTER BRISTOL

BATH

N. SOMERSET

AROUND

ACROSS

TOP FIVES

Fascinating Facts

⭐ Paddle steamers were the first type of powered boat, and the oldest ones appeared as early as 2,000 years ago, during Roman times. They were powered by oxen, or by slaves. Sadly paddle steamers aren't really used much any more as they're just not as good as some of the alternatives.

⭐ The Plimsoll line is painted on the outside of a ship to show how heavily loaded it is. A ship with a weighty cargo will sink lower into the water and so less of the line is visible. The Plimsoll line was invented in Bristol, and has been credited with saving hundreds of sailors' lives as ships that are not overloaded are less likely to sink.

⭐ Other famous inventions from Bristol include Ribena and Tarmac!

PLAN YOUR VISIT 18

Waverley Paddle Steamer

Sails from Cumberland Basin, Clevedon Pier and Weston-super-Mare

www.waverleyexcursions.co.uk

📞 0845 130 4647

££ – £££

I want to go here ☐

Top Tip

Children travel free on selected sailings. There's also a special kids' cruise day every summer.

Why are pirates so bad? They just arrrrrrrr!

WALK AROUND A TRACTOR GRAVEYARD

...at Oakham Treasures

Tell your parents that you want to collect stamps or toys, and they'll probably be happy. Tell them you want to collect tractors, and we reckon you'll have more trouble persuading them!

Luckily Keith Sherrell, the owner of Oakham Treasures, did decide to do just that. He now owns over 150 old and disused tractors which he's lovingly put on display in this museum. It's like a graveyard for tractors!

What's more, having got the taste for collecting, Keith didn't stop with tractors. He then moved on to 'other stuff'. As a result, this excellent museum is crowded with loads of historical curiosities including a re-created sweet shop, a hardware store, a haberdashery and a chemist. So clearly the tractors are just one factor!

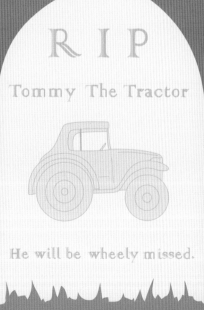

R I P

Tommy The Tractor

He will be wheely missed.

Sticker Scores

| 5 | 4 | 3 |
| TOP TRACTOR | CRACKING CART | PASSABLE PLOUGH |

| 2 | 1 |
| LAUGHABLE LAWNMOWER | PROTRACTOR |

CENTRAL BRISTOL

OUTER BRISTOL

BATH

N. SOMERSET

AROUND

ACROSS

TOP FIVES

Best Of The Rest

🔑 Stock up in the farm shop. Oakham is also a working farm, and in their shop you can buy home-cooked pies, cheese, hams and locally grown fruit and vegetables.

Photo Op

Many of the tractors at Oakham Treasures are lined up in neat rows. See how many tractors you can fit into the same photo!

Did you hear about the Magic Tractor? It turned into a field!

Fascinating Facts

⭐ **The word tractor comes from the Latin word *trahere*, meaning to pull. That's because tractors are mostly used by farmers to pull ploughs and make fields ready for planting seeds.**

⭐ For some, ploughing is not just work; it's also a sport! Every year the British National Ploughing Championships are held to see who can plough the best. The winner goes on to represent the UK at the World Ploughing Contest.

⭐ **Ploughs are thought to be more than 6,000 years old. Before tractors were invented they were pulled by oxen, camels, horses and even elephants! Sadly however, Keith doesn't have any elephants or camels in his museum.**

PLAN YOUR VISIT 19

Oakham Treasures

Oakham Farm, Portbury Lane, Portbury, BS20 7SP

www.oakhamtreasures.co.uk

📞 **01275 375 236**

🕐 **Tue-Sat 10.00-17.00**

££

I want to go here ☐

PICK YOUR OWN STRAWBERRIES

...at Chosen Hill Farm

We like fruit, and we think it tastes best when you've picked it yourself! At Chosen Hill Farm you can do just that . . . but you'll need all your self-control to stop yourself munching it as you go around!

Chosen Hill is a family run farm that allows you to pick your own fruit. You go into the fields to gather your chosen crop and then return to the shop so they can weigh and you can pay. There are loads of fruits to choose from including strawberries, raspberries, gooseberries and blackcurrants.

While you're picking, think about how to use the fruit. Make some jam, bake a fruit tart, or just eat it fresh. We're feeling hungry just thinking about it!

Sticker Scores

5 SUCCULENT STRAWBERRY

4 GORGEOUS GOOSEBERRY

3 BRILLIANT BLACKBERRY

2 AVERAGE APPLE

1 BLOW A RASPBERRY

CENTRAL BRISTOL

OUTER BRISTOL

BATH

N. SOMERSET

AROUND

ACROSS

TOP FIVES

Best Of The Rest

 There are plenty of pick-your-own places across the region, offering fruit, veg and even flowers. Here are two of the best (details can be found on www.pickyourownfarms.org.uk).

Poplars Farm is in Frampton Cotterell and also has a café on site.

Druid Farm is near to Stanton Drew Stone Circle (see p88) so you can combine both in a day trip.

Top Tip

Take a picnic to accompany your freshly picked fruit. Chosen Hill's farm shop also sells meringues, cream and ice creams to accompany your meal.

Fascinating Facts

★ **Strawberries are the only fruit with seeds on the outside. Each strawberry is covered with about 200 seeds.**

★ Around 27,000 kilogrammes of strawberries are eaten during the Wimbledon Tennis Championships. That's the same weight as 1,800 bales of straw (though the strawberries taste better)!

★ **In Belgium there's a museum dedicated to strawberries! The Strawberry Museum contains five rooms of strawberry-related exhibits. We're *berry* keen on visiting!**

Photo Op

Snap yourself stuffing your face with your fresh fruit. Just make sure you've paid for it first!

PLAN YOUR VISIT 20

Chosen Hill Farm

Hollowbrook Lane, Chew Magna, Somerset, BS40 8TH

www.chosenhillfarm.com

📞 **01275 332 397**

🕐 **May to August, call ahead for availability**

£ – **££**

I want to go here ☐

BATH

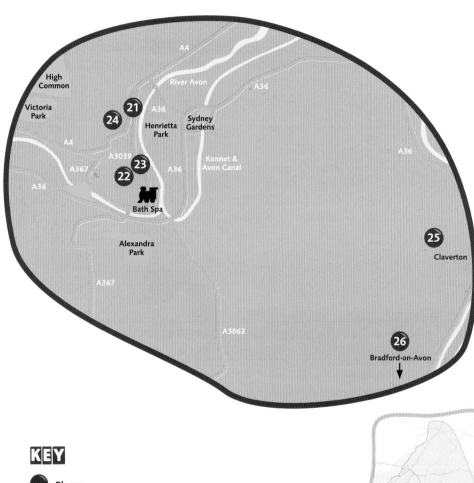

High
Common

Victoria
Park

River Avon

A4

A36

21

24

A36

Henrietta
Park

Sydney
Gardens

A36

A4

A3039

A367

23

22

A36

Kennet &
Avon Canal

A36

A36

Bath Spa

Alexandra
Park

25

Claverton

A367

A3062

26

Bradford-on-Avon

KEY

● Places

▮ Parks

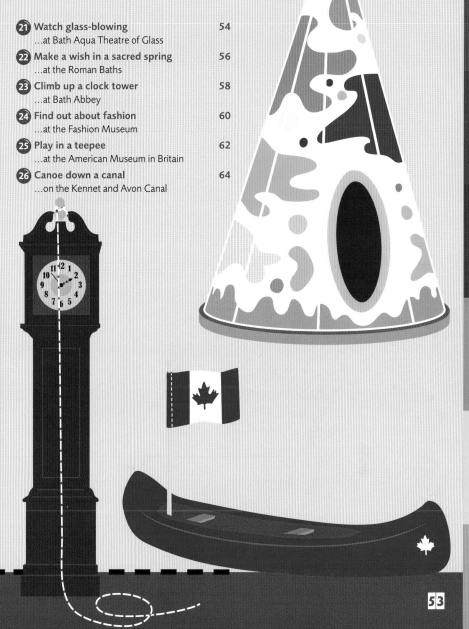

CENTRAL BRISTOL

OUTER BRISTOL

BATH

N. SOMERSET

AROUND

ACROSS

TOP FIVES

WATCH GLASS-BLOWING

...at Bath Aqua Theatre of Glass

If you blow on glass normally, not much happens. However, if the glass is hot enough when you blow on it, you can create all types of interesting shapes . . .

Glass-blowing is an ancient technique used to form shapes such as glasses and vases by blowing into a blob of glass so hot that it is almost liquid. When the glass cools down, it keeps its shape. It's a bit like blowing a soap bubble, only more dangerous!

Sticker Scores

5 GLASS-BLOWING

4 GLASS HOUSE

3 GLASS NOODLES

2 GLASS JUG

1 BROKEN GLASS

Bath Aqua Theatre of Glass offers regular glass-blowing demonstrations throughout the day. You get to see objects being moulded at around 1,000 degrees centigrade, and for an extra fee you even have the option to blow a glass bubble yourself!

CENTRAL BRISTOL

OUTER BRISTOL

BATH

N. SOMERSET

AROUND

ACROSS

TOP FIVES

Best Of The Rest

🔑 Gawp at the glass collection. Bath Aqua has lots on display – some Roman glass, a 150 year old stained-glass window and other bits of glass from all over Britain.

🔑 Check out the wall of fame, which contains glass hand casts of famous people.

← A glass-blowing furnace

What did the stained-glass window say to its child?
Stop being such a pane!

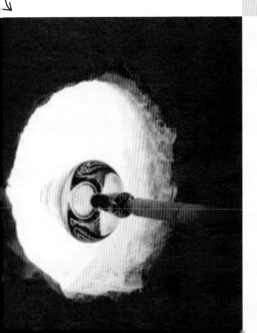

Fascinating Facts

⭐ Glass objects were probably first made about 3,500 years ago, but the invention of glass-blowing 1,500 years later allowed people to make larger and more complex things.

⭐ Surprisingly, glass is mostly made of sand. It also contains limestone, salt and ash. Sadly you can't just mix them together at home and make a vase – you need super-hot temperatures to melt the ingredients!

⭐ Glass can be formed naturally when meteorites or lightning collide with earth that contains the right substances! Tektite is the name for glass made by meteorites, and fulgurite the name for lightning glass. However, we don't recommend you try to watch either being formed, unless you want to be squished!

PLAN YOUR VISIT 21

Bath Aqua Theatre of Glass
105-107 Walcot Street, Bath, BA1 5BW
www.bathaquaglass.com

📞 **01225 428 146**

🕐 **Mon-Sat: demonstrations at 11.15 and 14.15
Call in advance for Saturdays as often privately booked**

£ 🎁

I want to go here ☐

MAKE A WISH IN A SACRED SPRING

...at the Roman Baths

Nowadays, baths are a dull (but necessary) part of the day. However, the Romans loved baths so much that the city is named after them!

The Roman Baths in Bath are heated by a natural hot spring which comes from deep within the earth's crust. Romans believed that it was created by the ancient gods, so they built a temple here and used it as a sacred spot to bathe.

During your visit you'll see their impressive pools and also have a chance to throw a coin into one of them and make a wish. Just don't bother bringing a bath-time rubber ducky – you're not allowed in the water!

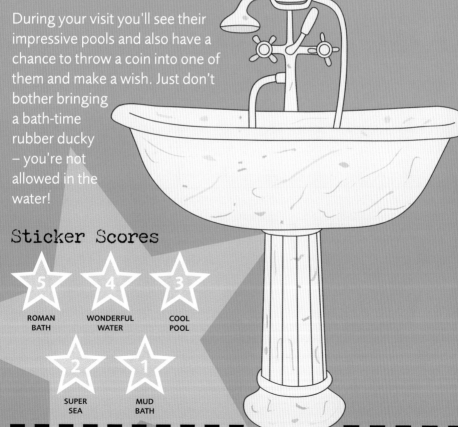

Sticker Scores

5 ROMAN BATH

4 WONDERFUL WATER

3 COOL POOL

2 SUPER SEA

1 MUD BATH

CENTRAL BRISTOL

OUTER BRISTOL

BATH

N. SOMERSET

AROUND

ACROSS

TOP FIVES

Best Of The Rest

🔑 Drink actual spa water in the Pump Room restaurant! It's open throughout the day, but can get quite busy so you may need to book ahead.

Top Tip

Combine your visit with a trip to the Fashion Museum (see p60) – it's cheaper to buy tickets for both at the same time.

Why did Julius Caesar buy crayons?
He wanted to Mark Antony!

Fascinating Facts

⭐ When the water bubbles to the surface at the Roman Baths its temperature is 46 degrees centigrade. That's hotter than normal bath water (but less likely to contain bubble bath)!

⭐ The Romans built a temple at the baths to honour the goddess Sulis Minerva. People thought she would help against their enemies, so they threw curses into one of the pools on small pieces of lead. Many were written in code to make sure that only Minerva could read them.

⭐ Romans didn't just bathe in the baths – they also used them as a big social centre. People would play ball games, eat, drink and get massaged here. Think of them as a cross between a swimming pool, a gym, a pub and a football pitch!

PLAN YOUR VISIT 22

Roman Baths

Abbey Churchyard, Bath, BA1 1LZ

www.romanbaths.co.uk

📞 01225 477 785

🕐 Daily (peak) 09.00-22.00
Daily (out of season) 09.30-17.30
Times vary from month to month

££

I want to go here ☐

CLIMB UP A CLOCK TOWER

...at Bath Abbey

Usually you only look at clocks from the front, because otherwise it's a bit tricky to tell the time. At Bath Abbey, however, you can actually get in behind the clock face by climbing up the tower!

There has been an abbey here since 757 A.D., but the current church is actually the third building to occupy the site and was only completed in 1611. It's a pretty awesome construction and can hold up to 1,200 people.

We particularly like the tower tours. You'll stand on top of the abbey's ceiling, hear and see the church bells up close, and take in the amazing view from the top of the tower. You also get to sit right behind the massive clock face!

Sticker Scores

⭐ 5
BIG BEN

⭐ 4
GRANDFATHER CLOCK

⭐ 3
WRISTWATCH

⭐ 2
STOPWATCH

⭐ 1
STOPPED WATCH

Sitting behind the clock face

Fascinating Facts

★ In October 2008, the city council put the abbey's clock back to winter time during the day (instead of at night, when clocks are usually changed). This caused a lot of confusion for the locals!

★ Tunes played by church bells are never allowed to have the same two notes in a row. That's because each bell needs time to stop vibrating before being bonged again.

★ The abbey's tenor bell weighs a whopping 1,688 kilogrammes. That's as much as a medium-sized car!

What's brown and sounds like a bell?

Dung!

Top Tip

For an awesome and amusing evening excursion, take a Bizarre Bath tour. They leave at 8 p.m. from the Huntsman Inn on North Parade Passage (daily March–October).

PLAN YOUR VISIT

Bath Abbey

12 Kingston Buildings, Bath, BA1 1LT

www.bathabbey.org

☏ 01225 422 462

🕐 Mon-Sat (summer): tours half-hourly 10.00-16.00
Mon-Sat (winter): tours at 11.00, 12.00, 14.00
Tours dependent on other events

I want to go here ☐

CENTRAL BRISTOL

OUTER BRISTOL

BATH

N. SOMERSET

AROUND

ACROSS

TOP FIVES

FIND OUT ABOUT FASHION

...at the Fashion Museum

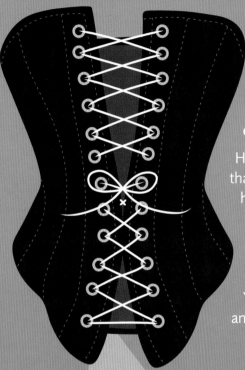

Fashion changes every season (and sometimes more frequently than that!) so it's appropriate that the Fashion Museum changes its exhibitions all the time too.

However, what you can rely on is that there will be a whole range of highly fashionable clothes from the last 300 years on show. Their collection contains everything from embroidered silk dresses and corsets to the latest designs. You'll also always find shoes, hats and bags on display.

Make sure you check out the Dress of the Year. Every year since 1963, someone influential in the world of fashion has chosen a dress to sum up the fashion vibe at the time. We think the museum's perfect for people with a passion for fashion!

Sticker Scores

5 — SMART SUIT

4 — SKIRT SUIT

3 — SHELL SUIT

2 — BIRTHDAY SUIT

1 — SUIT YOURSELF

CENTRAL BRISTOL
OUTER BRISTOL
BATH
N. SOMERSET
AROUND
ACROSS
TOP FIVES

Best Of The Rest

🔑 Visit the dressing-up section, where you can try on reproduction corsets and Victorian sporting clothes. There's football gear for the boys and archery stuff for the girls.

Top Tip

Make sure you pick up the trail for kids (complete with stickers) which is available at the front desk. You'll want to *stick-er* round to finish it!

Photo Op

Snap yourself in the dressing-up section wearing some of the traditional children's clothes.

← Dressing up

Fascinating Facts

⭐ Most lipsticks contain fish scales in the ingredients! That's because the scales give the lipstick a pearly sheen.

⭐ Apparently it was Napoleon, the famous French general, who started the trend for putting buttons on the sleeves of men's suit jackets. He ordered them to be sewn on his soldiers' uniforms to stop them wiping their runny noses on their clothes!

⭐ False eyebrows made out of mouse skin were a fashionable adornment worn by ladies in the 1700s. Thankfully, these days nobody thinks that accessories made from mice look nice!

What do you get if you cross a kangaroo and a sheep?
A woolly jumper!

PLAN YOUR VISIT 24

Fashion Museum
Assembly Rooms, Bennett Street, Bath, BA1 2QH
www.museumofcostume.co.uk

📞 **01225 477 789**

🕐 **Daily (summer) 10.30-18.00**
Daily (out of season) 10.30-17.00

££

I want to go here ☐

PLAY IN A TEEPEE

...at the American Museum in Britain

American Indians once used teepees as kitchens, bedrooms and playrooms. At the American Museum in Britain you'll sample what life was like for the Native Americans . . . not by cooking or sleeping in a teepee, but by playing in one!

The American Museum in Britain contains all kinds of interesting objects, such as American Indian moccasins and a bearskin rug. What's more, there's also plenty to do. You can dress up as a cowboy or try old games, like shove ha'penny, in a re-created tavern. Make sure you also leave time to play in the museum's gardens – check out the terrific teepee then run among the traditional American trees. It's an in-*tents* experience!

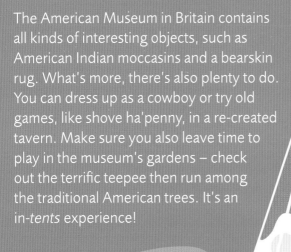

Sticker Scores

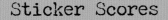

5 TERRIFIC TEEPEE

4 MAGNIFICENT MUD HUT

3 INTERESTING IGLOO

2 SATISFYING STRAW HUT

1 LEAKY LEAN-TO

CENTRAL BRISTOL

OUTER BRISTOL

BATH

N. SOMERSET

AROUND

ACROSS

TOP FIVES

Best Of The Rest

🔑 Go to a summer outdoor music event. You can picnic on the lawn, and even bring the family dog (on a lead).

🔑 See the Christmas decorations during December. There's also a Christmas trail to help you spot interesting stuff.

🔑 Check out the traditional craft shop or buy an ice cream. *Mmm!*

Top Tip
Bring a football or a Frisbee to play with on the museum's lawns.

Photo Op
Get a snap with you poking your head out of the entrance to a teepee!

AWAWAWAWA!

Fascinating Facts

⭐ Native Americans are the people who were living in America before it was colonised from the 1500s onwards. They had been living there for thousands of years before the arrival of Europeans caused their population to decline dramatically. This was largely because the newcomers brought strange diseases, started wars and made some Native Americans their slaves. Thankfully, when Europeans go on holiday these days they are better behaved!

⭐ Teepees are the cone-shaped tents that Native Americans used as their homes. They were usually made of animal skin or tree bark. They were NOT made of tea and pee!

PLAN YOUR VISIT 25

American Museum in Britain
Claverton Manor, Bath, BA2 7BD
www.americanmuseum.org

📞 **01225 460 503**

🕐 Tue-Sun (summer) 12.00-17.00
Opening hours vary throughout year

££

I want to go here ☐

CANOE DOWN A CANAL

...on the Kennet and Avon Canal

If you were taking a boat to Canada we wouldn't recommend a Canadian canoe. They wobble, they don't protect you from the weather and you can only paddle on one side at a time. Mind you, they are great fun for a day out on a canal!

A Canadian canoe is a small boat that's pointy at both ends. You can fit three to four people in one canoe, so they're fantastic for families. Hire one from TT Cycles, next to The Lock Inn, on the Kennet and Avon canal.

Sticker Scores

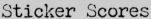

⭐ 5 — CRACKING CANOEIST

⭐ 4 — COMPETENT KAYAKER

⭐ 3 — PROFICIENT PADDLER

⭐ 2 — ROTTEN ROWER

⭐ 1 — CAPSIZED!

The boats also have flat bottoms which makes them harder to capsize. And after sitting in one for a few hours you might have a flat bottom too!

CENTRAL BRISTOL

OUTER BRISTOL

BATH

N. SOMERSET

AROUND

ACROSS

TOP FIVES

Best Of The Rest

🔑 Hire a bike. TT Cycles also hires out bikes for cycling on the Kennet and Avon Canal towpath. It's ten miles to Bath and twelve miles to Devizes along pleasantly flat paths!

Similar Spots

🔑 The Bath Boating Station also offers boat trips. You can hire old-style rowing boats, skiffs and punts for a relaxing day on the river Avon. www.bathboating.co.uk

Photo Op

Get the grown-ups to hold the canoe and take a picture of you standing up in the middle of it. Grab one of their hands if you think you might be about to fall in!

Fascinating Facts

⭐ **The longest canoe in the world is the Aries Punnamada Chundan, an Indian snake boat. It carries up to 141 people and is an impressive 43 metres long. That's the same as 25 Canadian men laid end to end!**

⭐ Canoes have traditionally been made out of a variety of stuff, such as hollowed logs or animal skins. American Indians developed particularly impressive canoes partly because they had no horses, so they needed to find other ways of travelling and transporting heavy things.

PLAN YOUR VISIT 26

TT Cycles

48 Frome Road, Bradford on Avon, Wiltshire, BA15 1LE

www.towpathtrail.co.uk

📞 **01225 867 187**

🕐 **Daily 09.00-18.00**

££

I want to go here ☐

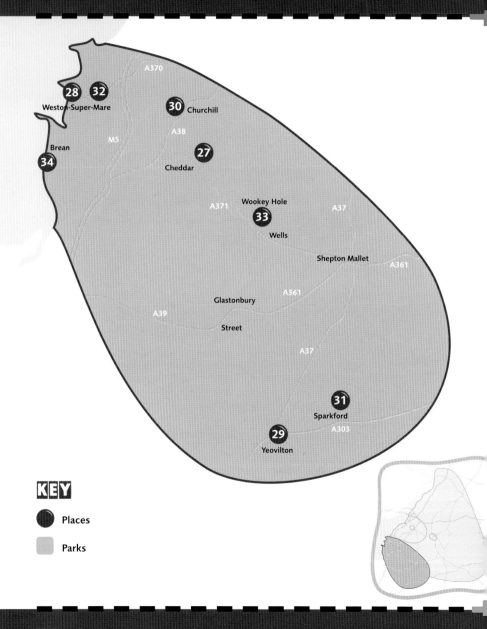

A370

28 32
Weston-Super-Mare

30 Churchill

A38

Brean

34

27
Cheddar

M5

Wookey Hole

A371 33 A37

Wells

Shepton Mallet

A361

A361

Glastonbury

A39

Street

A37

31
Sparkford

29 A303

Yeovilton

KEY

⬤ Places

▢ Parks

MUSEUM

HOTAY

CENTRAL BRISTOL

OUTER BRISTOL

BATH

N. SOMERSET

AROUND

ACROSS

TOP FIVES

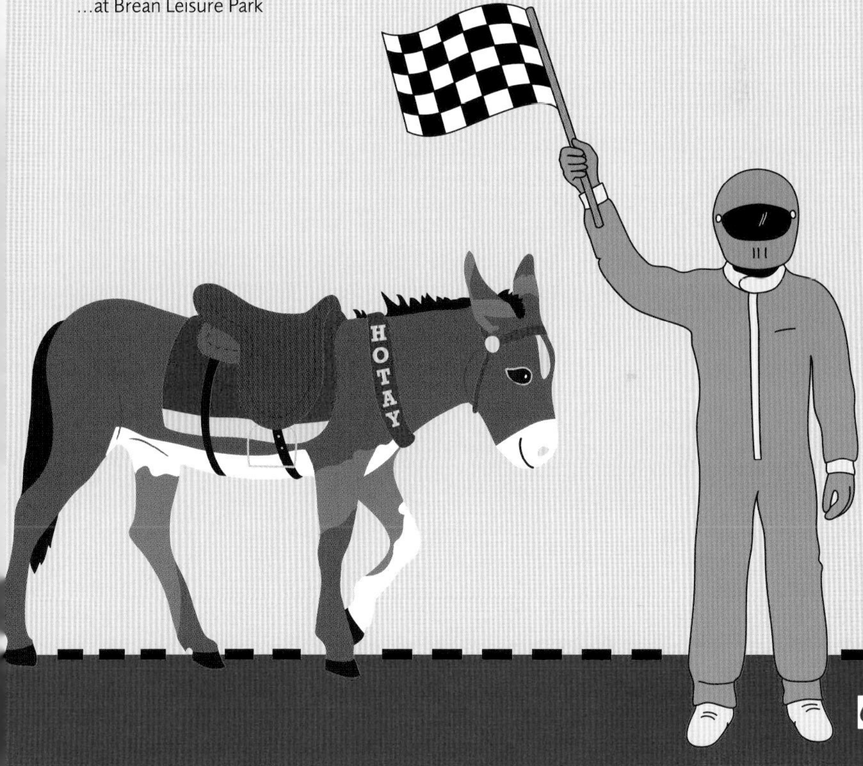

GO ON A CRYSTAL QUEST

...at Cheddar Caves

Despite the name, Cheddar Caves are not made out of cheese. In fact they are a network of seriously cool underground caves!

Start off in Cox's Cave, where you'll find marvellous mirror pools and curiously coloured stalagmites and stalactites. It also contains the Crystal Quest – a fantastic fantasy adventure where you can help rescue the crystal of light from the lord of darkness, passing elves, warriors and smoke-breathing dragons along the way.

After capturing the crystal, head to Gough's Cave to see a 13,000 year old drawing of a mammoth. You'll also find the UK's largest colony of endangered greater horseshoe bats . . . and some cheddar cheese. You'd *brie* mad not to visit!

Sticker Scores

5 CHEDDAR CHEESE

4 CHEESE ON TOAST

3 CHEESE AND PICKLE

2 CHEESE SLICE

1 CHEESED OFF

CENTRAL BRISTOL

OUTER BRISTOL

BATH

N. SOMERSET

AROUND

ACROSS

TOP FIVES

Best Of The Rest

 Climb the 274 steps up Jacob's Ladder, a steep stairway in the side of the gorge. You'll need to tackle a further 48 steps to get to the viewing platform – but the view's worth the walk.

 Make your own cave painting in the Museum of Prehistory. During the summer you can also see prehistoric people (or rather, actors in fancy dress) showing how they used to light fires.

Top Tip

While you need a Cave and Gorge Explorer ticket to get into all the attractions mentioned on this page, it's completely free to walk up the gorge.

Fascinating Facts

★ **The oldest complete human skeleton in Britain was found in Cheddar. He is known as Cheddar Man and is about 9,000 years old.**

★ Cannibalism is thought to have been common amongst prehistoric humans. In the Museum of Prehistory you'll see the remains of people who appear to have been eaten. We'd rather chomp on a cheese sandwich!

★ **Unsurprisingly, cheddar cheese was invented in Cheddar. Though most cheddar is now made elsewhere, some is still made locally and stored in the caves.**

Which is the best cheese to hide a small horse in? *Mask-a-pony!*

PLAN YOUR VISIT 27

Cheddar Caves & Gorge
Cheddar, Somerset, BS27 3QF
www.cheddarcaves.co.uk

 01934 742 343

Daily (summer) 10.00-17.30
Daily (out of season) 10.30-17.00

£££

I want to go here ☐

RIDE A DONKEY

...on the beach at Weston-super-Mare

Riding a donkey isn't difficult. They're smaller than horses and generally quite friendly. So it's unlikely that you'll fall off and make an *ass* of yourself!

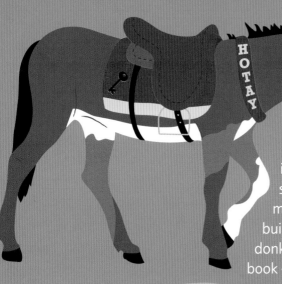

Weston-super-Mare beach is one of the longest and sandiest in the UK. That makes it superb for sandcastle building and delightful for donkey riding! There's no need to book – just turn up at the beach on a summer day and the donkeys will be there waiting for you.

As well as donkeys, you'll find loads of other attractions along the seafront like roundabouts, swing boats, a bouncy castle and even a miniature railway. We're sure you'll agree it's a peach of a beach!

Sticker Scores

5 GOLDEN SAND

4 PEBBLE BEACH

3 ROCKY SHORE

2 CLIFF FACE

1 QUICKSAND

CENTRAL BRISTOL

OUTER BRISTOL

BATH

N. SOMERSET

AROUND

ACROSS

TOP FIVES

Make A Day Of It

🔑 Visit the pier. Weston's Grand Pier was destroyed by a fire in 2008 but they managed to rebuild it in just two years so it's now open again. www.grandpierwsm.co.uk

🔑 Take a whirl on the Wheel of Weston. This 40 metre high observation wheel gives a spectacular view of the surrounding area. On a clear day you can see Wales (but sadly no whales)!

🔑 See sharks at the aquarium! The Weston SeaQuarium has an amazing underwater tunnel and open-top tanks, plus feeding sessions throughout the day. www.seaquarium.co.uk

Fascinating Facts

⭐ **The Mager family have offered donkey rides on Weston-super-Mare beach for more than 100 years. Their donkeys are well cared for: only children up to the age of fourteen are allowed to ride them so they are never overworked.**

⭐ Weston-super-Mare hosts a sand-sculpture event every year. During the summer, sculptors from around the world make incredible creations out of sand.

⭐ **A mule is a cross between a donkey and a horse. An ass is another name for a wild donkey (or a fool!).**

Photo Op

Draw the outline of a speedboat in the sand, dig out the seating area and get someone to take a photo of you sitting in it.

PLAN YOUR VISIT 28

Weston-super-Mare beach

Somerset

www.westondonkeys.co.uk

📞 01934 813 769

🕐 Daily (summer only)

£

I want to go here ☐

EXPLORE AN AIRCRAFT CARRIER

...at the Fleet Air Arm Museum

Aircraft carriers are enormous ships which are used to launch fighter jets. That means they're much too big to fit inside a museum, but the Fleet Air Arm has got round this by re-creating one inside a huge hangar.

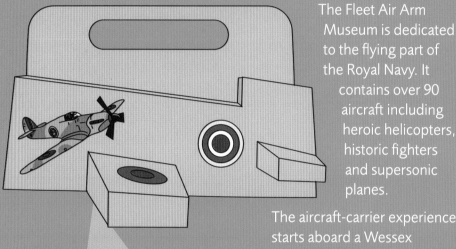

The Fleet Air Arm Museum is dedicated to the flying part of the Royal Navy. It contains over 90 aircraft including heroic helicopters, historic fighters and supersonic planes.

The aircraft-carrier experience starts aboard a Wessex helicopter. Huge movie screens make you feel like you're landing on the HMS *Ark Royal* while powerful fighter jets take off around you. Once on board you tour the ship's control rooms and cabins, and even get to see a nuclear bomb! Trust us – you'll want to *hangar*-ound!

Sticker Scores

5 TOP GUN

4 FIGHTER PILOT

3 REAR GUNNER

2 COMMERCIAL CAPTAIN

1 PLANE STUPID

Best Of The Rest

🔑 Check out the Concorde! The Fleet Air Arm is home to the first British-built Concorde. It was the only commercial aircraft that could fly at twice the speed of sound. (See p34 for another cracking Concorde.)

🔑 Take a trail in search of toy animals. Some aircraft contain toy versions of the creatures they are named after!

🔑 Test yourself on the Mini Marines assault course, just next to the Swordfish restaurant.

← Mainly a fun museum!

Photo Op

Get a snap of you in front of your favourite aircraft with your arms stretched out like plane wings. There are tons to choose from!

Fascinating Facts

⭐ Aircraft carriers aren't cheap. The USS *George H. W. Bush*, for example, was bought by the US Army in 2009 for four billion pounds. That's enough money to buy around 2,300 private jets!

Top Tip

Check out the museum's holiday activities schedule. At one of the sessions you can make a parachute. Once you're done, attach it to an egg and drop the chute from the back of Concorde. If your parachute is good enough, the egg won't break!

PLAN YOUR VISIT

Fleet Air Arm Museum

Yeovilton, Ilchester, Somerset, BA22 8HT

www.fleetairarm.com

 01935 840 565

 Daily (summer) 10.00-17.30
Wed-Sun (out of season) 10.00-16.30

I want to go here ☐

SKI DOWN A HILL

...at Avon Ski and Action Centre

Bristol wouldn't be your first choice for a skiing holiday. There aren't any mountains for one thing, and it also rarely snows. However, that doesn't mean it's a ski-free city, because you can still slide down a hill at the Avon dry ski slope!

Dry skiing is a great way of learning how to ski without having to travel outside England. The slope is made up of small plastic bristles which you slide over. It's a bit like skiing on a giant hairbrush!

You can hire equipment by the hour if you visit with expert skiers. Alternatively, newcomers can book ahead to have a lesson. And if you don't feel like skiing, there's tobogganing down the slope each hour. It's great fun, and that's *snow* joke!

Sticker Scores

5 SUPERB SKIS

4 SNAZZY SNOWBOARD

3 LUXURY LUGE

2 TERRIFYING TOBOGGAN

1 TEA TRAY

CENTRAL BRISTOL

OUTER BRISTOL

BATH

N. SOMERSET

AROUND

ACROSS

TOP FIVES

Similar Spots

🔑 There's another great dry ski slope in Gloucester. The Gloucester Ski & Snowboard Centre is about an hour north of Bristol, near the M5 motorway. www.gloucesterski.com

Best Of The Rest

🔑 The Avon Ski and Action Centre has lots going on besides the skiing. Other activities include archery, rifle shooting, mountainboarding, rock climbing, abseiling and power kiting. Some age and height restrictions apply, so check the website for details before you visit.

Fascinating Facts

⭐ The sport of ski jumping involves sliding down a steep ramp before being launched into the air at the bottom. The world record is held by a Norwegian called Bjørn Einar Romøren, who jumped a whopping 239 metres. That's like leaping across nine standard-sized swimming pools!

Top Tip

If you're feeling peckish, head to the Crown Inn, a lovely traditional pub which is a five-minute drive from the ski slope. It's our favourite local spot to munch on some lunch!

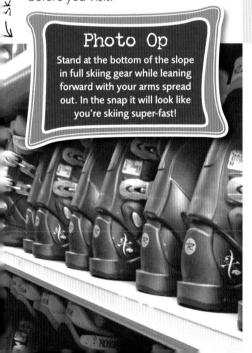

Photo Op

Stand at the bottom of the slope in full skiing gear while leaning forward with your arms spread out. In the snap it will look like you're skiing super-fast!

← ski shoes

PLAN YOUR VISIT 30

Avon Ski and Action Centre

Lyncombe Drive, Churchill, North Somerset, BS25 5PQ

www.avonski.co.uk

📞 01934 852 335

🕐 Mon-Fri 09.00-20.00
Sat-Sun 09.00-18.00

£££

I want to go here ☐

DRIVE A GO-KART

...at Haynes International Motor Museum

Here's a place that has not one but TWO ways to drive a go-kart! First, there's an awesome go-kart simulator inside the museum . . . and then there's also a great go-kart track outside!

The Haynes International Motor Museum is home to over 400 amazing cars, motorbikes and military vehicles. And there's loads to do besides gawping at the marvellous motors!

Head to the Cycraft simulator for a video game karting experience. You choose a kart, then race it while strapped into the futuristic machine. Or, if you feel like the real thing, head to the kids' race track where you can whizz around in a battery-powered kart. We suggest you make *v-room* in your schedule for a visit!

Sticker Scores

5 GO-KART

4 HORSE AND CART

3 DODGEM

2 BICYCLE

1 GO HOME

CENTRAL BRISTOL

OUTER BRISTOL

BATH

N. SOMERSET

AROUND

ACROSS

TOP FIVES

Best Of The Rest

🔑 Visit the interactive displays where you can see how an engine works.

🔑 Take control of a digger and pick up some sand in the Super Diggers section.

🔑 Clamber around the outside adventure play area, or hang out in the fun bus, which contains a soft play area.

← Look out Lewis Hamilton!

Photo Op

Get a snap of you with a real Formula One car that used to be driven by Michael Schumacher. You can pose near the car for free, or inside it for a fee.

Fascinating Facts

★ The museum's Red Room contains over 50 superb sports cars from around the world . . . and every single one is black! (OK, we're lying about the last bit. They're all red.)

★ The current land-speed record is an astonishing 763 mph. That's faster than the speed of sound! It was set by Andy Green in 1997, in a British-designed car (but not on a motorway).

Top Tip

Hold a competition with your family and friends to see who can find the oldest, fastest and biggest car on display.

PLAN YOUR VISIT 31

Haynes International Motor Museum

Sparkford, Yeovil, Somerset, BA22 7LH

www.haynesmotormuseum.com

📞 **01963 440 804**

🕐 **Daily (summer) 09.30-17.30 or 18.00 Daily (out of season) 10.00-16.30**

££*

*some exhibits have additional charges

I want to go here ☐

CHECK OUT SOME CHOPPERS

...at the Helicopter Museum

On most days, the only chopper you're likely to see is somebody slicing up vegetables. So a visit to the Helicopter Museum is a bit of a treat, because they've got a collection of over 80 helicopters from around the world. That's our kind of chopper!

The Helicopter Museum's collection contains everything from the Queen's helicopter to a Russian gunship, all stored in huge hangars. We particularly like the Bensen Gyro-Boat – a cross between a wooden dinghy and a two-blade helicopter! Now that would be a great way of getting to school . . .

Sticker Scores

5	4	3
HEROIC HELICOPTER	CHAMPION CHINOOK	GREAT GYRO-COPTER

2	1
PAPER PLANE	SYCAMORE SEED

As well as helicopters, there's also helicopter film footage and an outside playground. Make sure you leave time to visit the shop which stocks a huge range of model helicopters (but sadly no Gyro-Boats!).

CENTRAL BRISTOL

OUTER BRISTOL

BATH

N. SOMERSET

AROUND

ACROSS

TOP FIVES

Top Tip

The museum has monthly open-cockpit days where you get to go inside the cockpits of the helicopters. Experienced guides show you how the controls work.

↙ A giraffe. Oh, OK, it's a helicopter!

Photo Op

Take a pic of you on the steps of the Queen's helicopter doing a royal wave!

Top Tip

Every May the museum hosts a big helicopter show. Helicopters arrive and depart all day, and you can test your piloting skills on over 40 flight simulators!

Fascinating Facts

⭐ The British Army's Apache Mark 1 helicopters cost around £40 million to buy, and around £30,000 per hour to fly! So sadly Santa is unlikely to bring you one this year . . .

⭐ Unlike aeroplanes, helicopters can fly up, down, backwards or forward. They're also able to hover on the spot. This makes them ideal for search-and-rescue operations because they can wait above people in trouble and land just about anywhere there's a bit of open space. Helicopters are thought to have saved over three million lives since the first person was rescued from the sea in 1944.

PLAN YOUR VISIT

The Helicopter Museum

Locking Moor Road, Weston-super-Mare, Somerset, BS24 8PP

www.helicoptermuseum.co.uk

📞 01934 635 227

🕐 Daily (summer) 10.00-17.30
Wed-Sun (out of season) 10.00-16.30

I want to go here ☐

FIND THE WITCH OF WOOKEY

...at Wookey Hole Caves

As far as we know, none of the other places in this book have a witch. And if they do, they're keeping quiet about it! However, Wookey Hole actually encourages you to search for their witch!

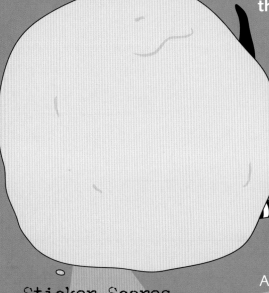

Wookey Hole is home to a series of beautiful, and slightly spooky, caves set in the limestone rock of the Mendip Hills. You can take a tour that leads you through several colourful and creepy chambers as you hunt for the cave-dwelling witch.

Apart from the cave tour, you can get lost in the mirror maze, play in a penny arcade or explore a miniature village. There's such a strange range of stuff to do on your visit you'll have a tough decision deciding *witch* to do first!

Sticker Scores

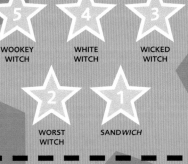

5	4	3
WOOKEY WITCH	WHITE WITCH	WICKED WITCH

2	1
WORST WITCH	SAND*WICH*

CENTRAL BRISTOL

OUTER BRISTOL

BATH

N. SOMERSET

AROUND

ACROSS

TOP FIVES

Best Of The Rest

See life-size dinos in the Valley of the Dinosaurs. There are over twenty models set along a walkway, from a terrifying T. rex to the vegetarian stegosaurus.

Top Tip

Wookey Hole is best to visit when it's sunny. Although it's well known for the caves, a surprising number of the attractions are outside.

Photo Op

For a prehistoric photo, take a snap of yourself next to a life-size dinosaur.

Fascinating Facts

★ The legend of the witch of Wookey Hole began over a thousand years ago. The witch was thought to be responsible for all the bad things that happened in the local village. Everyone feared her until a monk turned her to stone by throwing a bucket of holy water on her. *Wat-er* relief!

★ Confusingly, you can actually see *two* witches at Wookey Hole. The first is a stalagmite which looks a bit like a witch and is said to be the stony remains of the legendary sorceress. The second is the live witch that can be found lurking in the caves.

★ The UK's first ever rabbit wedding took place at the caves in April 2008. The world's largest bunny, Roberto, hopped down the aisle with Amy, who was wearing a veil.

PLAN YOUR VISIT 33

Wookey Hole Caves

Wookey Hole, Wells, Somerset, BA5 1BB

www.wookey.co.uk

📞 01749 672 243

🕐 Daily (summer) 10.00-17.00
Daily (out of season) 10.00-16.00

£££

I want to go here ☐

GO TO A FUN CITY

...at Brean Leisure Park

OK, Fun City is not an actual city, but it is definitely fun. In fact, it's even better than a real city because it's full of fairground rides!

Fun City is part of Brean Leisure Park, which is the largest amusement park in the South West. The rides include dodgems, roller-coasters, carousels, haunted houses and waltzers . . . in fact there are far too many to list them all! We particularly like the Wild Water Log Flume – it's *splash*-tastic!

And if that isn't enough fun for you, there's also a swimming pool (so don't forget your costume), and a pitch-and-putt golf course. Once you've *Brean*, you'll definitely want to go back!

Sticker Scores

5	4	3
FUNFAIR	FAIRGROUND	FAIR WEATHER

2	1
SUMMER FAIR	UNFAIR

CENTRAL BRISTOL

OUTER BRISTOL

BATH

N. SOMERSET

AROUND

ACROSS

TOP FIVES

Best Of The Rest

🔑 See a live show. Brean has a range of live performances on certain days of the year. There's everything from magic to fireworks!

🔑 Spot Sooty and Sweep. One of these popular TV puppets can be found walking around the park every day. Brean Leisure Park also hosts *The Sooty Show Live* – check the website for a schedule.

What do you get if you put a teddy bear in the freezer?

A teddy-*brrr*!

Fascinating Facts

⭐ Sooty is a yellow puppet bear who has been on television since the 1950s. He is friends with a dopey dog called Sweep and a pleasant panda called Soo. Sooty celebrated his 60th birthday by texting Nelson Mandela, the former President of South Africa. A video of Sooty sending his message can be seen on YouTube.

⭐ The longest roller-coaster in the world is at Nagashima Spa Land in Japan. It's called the Steel Dragon and is 1.5 miles long! That's longer than six laps of an Olympic running track.

Photo Op
Snap yourself screaming on the scariest ride you can find!

PLAN YOUR VISIT 34

Brean Leisure Park
Coast Road, Brean Sands, Somerset, TA8 2QY
www.funcitybrean.co.uk

📞 01278 751 595

🕐 Mar-Oct, times vary by season and by day

£££

I want to go here ☐

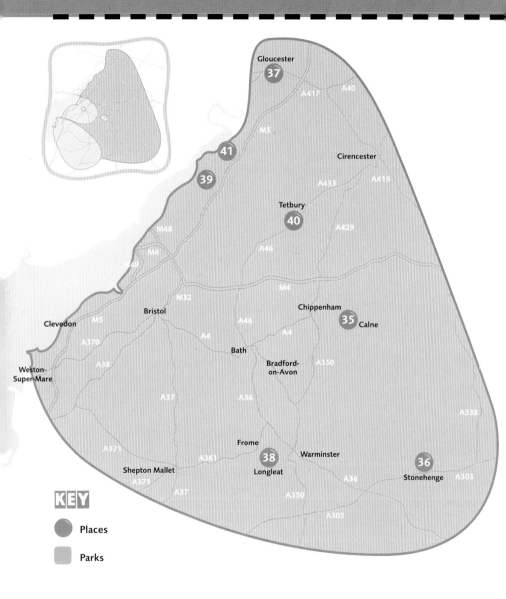

KEY

- 🔴 Places
- 🟦 Parks

CENTRAL BRISTOL

OUTER BRISTOL

BATH

N. SOMERSET

AROUND

ACROSS

TOP FIVES

DROP DOWN A DEATH SLIDE

...at Bowood House

Despite the description, death slides don't really involve any dying! Instead you whoosh down a steep slide, making your stomach lurch. And one of our favourite death slides is the Space Dive in Bowood's awesome adventure playground!

Bowood House is a large stately home. Adults visit for the rare antiques and glorious gardens. But we suggest you go to have fun. You'll find a full-sized pirate ship, aerial walkways and the Space Dive, which starts with a six-metre vertical drop. That's like falling from the roof of a two-storey building!

Sticker Scores

⭐ 5 — DEATH SLIDE

⭐ 4 — DEATH BY CHOCOLATE

⭐ 3 — DEATH VALLEY

⭐ 2 — DEATH METAL

⭐ 1 — DEATH

Our favourite way to go down the slide is to climb to the top, grab onto the metal bar, dangle over the edge and let go. It's *dead* scary!

CENTRAL BRISTOL

OUTER BRISTOL

BATH

N. SOMERSET

AROUND

ACROSS

TOP FIVES

Best Of The Rest

🔑 Stroll around the gorgeous gardens. There is an arboretum and a large lake. Visit in May or June and you'll also be able to walk through the blooming rhododendrons (a pretty flower).

Similar Spots

🔑 See p114 for five more amazing adventure playgrounds around Bristol and Bath.

Photo Op

Snap yourself standing in the crow's nest on the pirate ship. *Ahoy there, me hearties!*

Fascinating Facts

★ **The adventure playground is entirely constructed using timber from the Bowood estate. But then again, they *wood*!**

★ Bowood estate was bought in 1754 by the first Earl of Shelburne. His descendents still live there today, over 250 years later.

★ Death slide is a slightly confusing term. At Bowood, and many other adventure playgrounds, it's a slide which starts off steeply and gradually flattens out. In other places it refers to an aerial runway, where you hold on to a handle and slide down a long wire. Thankfully, neither involves any real death. *Phew!*

★ Singapore airport has a huge slide. It's twelve metres tall and keeps customers entertained before and after their flights.

PLAN YOUR VISIT 35

Bowood House
Derry Hill, Calne, Wiltshire, SN11 0LZ
www.bowood-house.co.uk

📞 **01249 812 102**

🕐 **Daily (summer) 11.00-17.00**

££

I want to go here ☐

SOLVE THE MYSTERY OF THE MEGALITHS

...at Stonehenge

Normally, the idea of some stones in a field would not be that exciting. However, we're not talking about just any set of rocks. We're referring to Stonehenge's startling stone circle!

Stonehenge was probably built around 5,000 years ago, during the Stone Age. However, no one knows how the megaliths (large stones) got there. Each one is huge and very heavy, so construction must have been incredibly complicated.

The other big mystery is what the megaliths were used for. There are all kinds of theories: some say it was a site for worshipping the sun; others say it was a place for healing or sacrifice. There's even a suggestion that it was once a sacred graveyard. Maybe you can come up with your own theory!

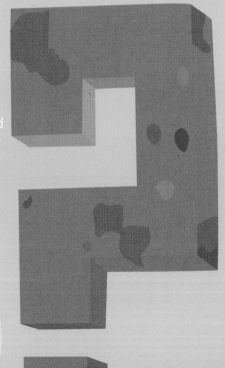

Sticker Scores

⭐ 5	⭐ 4	⭐ 3
STONEHENGE	STONE AGE	STONE STATUE

⭐ 2	⭐ 1
STONE COLD	STONE THE CROWS

CENTRAL BRISTOL

OUTER BRISTOL

BATH

N. SOMERSET

AROUND

ACROSS

TOP FIVES

Similar Spots

 Stanton Drew Stone Circle near Bristol is a much smaller and quieter stone circle. It's free to visit and you can even have a picnic in the middle of the stones!

 Avebury Stone Circle, nearby in Wiltshire, is one of Europe's largest. It's run by the National Trust and you can walk up to the circle for free.

Photo Op

Take a snap of you making a circle with your hands and standing in front of the famous stone circle!

Top Tip

You can book special Stone Circle Access visits which allow you to walk inside Stonehenge. They take place outside normal hours and need to be arranged at least a couple of weeks in advance.

Fascinating Facts

★ **The megaliths at Stonehenge are partially buried in the ground to make sure they don't topple over. The holes were probably dug using antlers and bones, so it would have been back-breaking work.**

★ Each megalith weighs between 20 and 50 tonnes. That's as heavy as 1,350 nine year olds!

★ **Each year, hundreds of people spend the night at Stonehenge to celebrate the summer solstice. This is a festival to mark the longest day in the year, which some people consider to be an important spiritual event.**

PLAN YOUR VISIT 36

Stonehenge
Nr Amesbury, SP4 7DE
www.english-heritage.org.uk

📞 0870 333 1181

🕐 Daily, times vary by month

££ ✗

I want to go here ☐

OPEN UP A MASSIVE LOCK

...at the National Waterways Museum

Getting into a lock might sound simple, providing you have the right key. But when you're talking about a canal lock containing hundreds of tonnes of water it becomes a bit more complicated!

Canal locks are ways of moving boats up and down hills. Canals have to be flat so that boats can go along them in either direction, so when things become hilly, locks act like water-filled steps. That might sound complicated, but the National Waterways Museum does a great job of explaining how the system works.

Our favourite bit is where you get to use a lock yourself. You can also have a boat race, or turn your hand to boat-building. *Wat-er-way* to spend a day!

Sticker Scores

5	4	3
YALE LOCK	D-LOCK	PADLOCK

2	1
COMBINATION LOCK	WARLOCK

CENTRAL BRISTOL

OUTER BRISTOL

BATH

N. SOMERSET

AROUND

ACROSS

TOP FIVES

Best Of The Rest

🔑 Take a boat trip on the canal. For an extra charge you can ride on board *Queen Boadicea II*, which was once used to rescue soldiers from the beaches of Dunkirk during World War Two.

🔑 Find out about canal wildlife, and discover what birds and fish you should look out for next time you're walking alongside a canal.

🔑 Practise pulling a pulley. Use all your strength to pick up a big sack using the museum's interactive pulley.

A canal boat

Fascinating Facts

⭐ A series of locks close together is referred to as a flight, just like a flight of stairs. There's a flight of sixteen locks at Caen Hill on the Kennet and Avon canal. That's a lot of opening and closing!

Photo Op

On the dockside there are loads of boats that you can climb aboard. Find your favourite and snap yourself standing on it while making a naval salute!

CYLGATE

PLAN YOUR VISIT 37

National Waterways Museum

Llanthony Warehouse, The Docks, Gloucester, GL1 2EH

www.nwm.org.uk/gloucester

📞 01452 318 200

🕐 Daily 11.00-16.00

£

I want to go here ☐

COME FACE TO FACE WITH A LION

...at Longleat Safari Park

Wiltshire is not the most obvious place to look at a lion. However, Longleat Safari Park is proof that you can get up close to one without going to Africa.

Longleat was the first safari park outside Africa, and it has been open since 1966. You drive your car through a series of parks filled with all sorts of animals you won't see at your average farm.

On your safari you trundle through Tiger Territory, wonder at Wolf Wood, gaze at giraffes and peer at pelicans. Our favourite bit is Lion Country, where the huge cats can come right up close to your car. Just don't get out to meet the lions, or you'll end up as lion food!

Sticker Scores

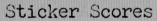

5	4	3
LONGLEAT LION	GORGEOUS GIRAFFE	PRETTY PELICAN

2	1
WICKED WOLF	SCAREDY-CAT

CENTRAL BRISTOL

OUTER BRISTOL

BATH

N. SOMERSET

AROUND

ACROSS

TOP FIVES

Best Of The Rest

🔑 Be a-*maze*-d by the Hedge Maze. It contains almost two miles of paths, so try not to get too lost!

🔑 Explore the adventure castle – an adventure playground in the shape of a castle.

🔑 Get even closer to the animals in the park's Animal Adventure section. If you're brave enough you can stand in a room full of free-flying bats!

Top Tip

Check out Longleat's Junior Rangers videos in the KidZone part of their website. The rangers go behind the scenes at the safari park, handle snakes and feed sea lions.

Fascinating Facts

⭐ **A group of lions is known as a pride. Presumably lions are rather pleased with themselves!**

⭐ Female lions do most of the pride's hunting. The lazy males spend their time *lyin'* around!

⭐ **The giraffe is one of the fastest animals in the world, with a top speed of around 35 mph. That's faster than the speed limit on many Wiltshire roads!**

⭐ A tiger's stripes are as unique as a human fingerprint – no two patterns look the same. Even if you shaved off all a tiger's fur the stripes would still be visible on its skin.

PLAN YOUR VISIT 38

Longleat Safari Park

Warminster, Wiltshire, BA12 7NW

www.longleat.co.uk

📞 **01985 844 4000**

🕐 **Opening hours vary – check website**

£££

I want to go here ☐

MARVEL AT A MEDIEVAL KEEP

...at Berkeley Castle

Berkeley Castle is over 900 years old, and was built to keep the Welsh out of the area. But don't worry if you're from Wales – these days they allow visitors from anywhere in the world!

Berkeley Castle is the oldest building in the country to have never changed hands – the Berkeleys have lived here since it was constructed! When you visit you can walk through the keep and imagine being a soldier defending it against intruders. You can also visit the kitchens, which contain ancient equipment that servants used to cook with. And don't miss the dungeon where King Edward II was imprisoned and murdered in 1327. We're sure you'll enjoy your visit more than Edward did!

Sticker Scores

5 CRACKING CASTLE

4 POSH PALACE

3 FASCINATING FORTRESS

2 MIDDLING MANSION

1 HOUSE OF CARDS

Top Tip

During the holidays Berkeley Castle hosts special events, including children's activity days and outdoor plays. Check the website for details.

CENTRAL BRISTOL

OUTER BRISTOL

BATH

N. SOMERSET

AROUND

ACROSS

TOP FIVES

Best Of The Rest

🔑 Flutter by the butterfly centre located in the gardens. The enclosure is home to the world's largest moth, the Atlas. Stay still and one might even land on you!

🔑 Explore the gardens, where you'll find a lovely lily pond and beautiful old orchards.

Make A Day Of It

🔑 The nearby Cattle Country Adventure Park has play areas, a willow maze, a bison-handling pen and the UK's largest climbing net.

Fascinating Facts

⭐ **Berkeley Castle's keep was built in the 1100s and contains clever features to make sure it was well-defended. These include trip steps to make the enemy stumble during an assault, murder holes, arrow loops and massive barred doors.**

⭐ The vaccine for smallpox was invented in 1796 by a man from Berkeley village called Edward Jenner. This horrific disease caused pimples all over the body and killed many of its victims. In 1979 the disease was finally eradicated – and Edward can take the credit for saving millions of lives.

PLAN YOUR VISIT 39

Berkeley Castle
Berkeley, Gloucestershire, GL13 9BQ
www.berkeley-castle.com

📞 **01453 810 332**

🕐 **Sun-Thu (summer) 11.00-17.30**
Open Fri and Sat during Easter

I want to go here ☐

PLAY HIDE-AND-SEEK IN A TREE MUSEUM

...at Westonbirt Arboretum

Say the word museum and you might think of a boring building with old things inside it. But a tree museum (or arboretum) is full of living trees, and it's great for a game of hide-and-seek!

Westonbirt Arboretum is a collection of over 3,000 different trees from around the world. Many are endangered in their own countries, so it's an important conservation collection. Speak to the staff in the information centre and see if they'll help you locate the biggest, the oldest and the rarest tree. They also have great children's trails, which show you where you can build a den and jump across tree stumps. It's a *tree*-mendous place!

Sticker Scores

⭐ 5
TOP TREE

⭐ 4
AMAZING ASH

⭐ 3
PLEASANT PINE

⭐ 2
ORDINARY OAK

⭐ 1
BARK-ING MAD

Best Of The Rest

🔑 Search for the 2,000-year-old lime tree in the Old Arboretum.

🔑 Buy some seeds from the on-site garden centre so you can go home and grow your own plants.

🔑 Munch on a cake from the outdoor café. The chocolate brownies are brilliant!

Top Tip

Visit during the autumn and you'll find a fantastic mix of colours in the arboretum. The Japanese maple garden becomes particularly pretty at this time of year.

Fascinating Facts

⭐ **The roots of a mature oak tree can extend underground to cover an area the size of a football pitch! Sadly, however, you can't really play football around one as the tree gets in the way.**

⭐ The tallest tree in the world is thought to be a redwood in California called Hyperion. It's around 115 metres tall, which is the same as 1,500 bonsai trees standing on top of each other!

⭐ **An average-sized tree contains enough wood to make 170,000 pencils! Though frankly we're not sure why anyone *wood* need that many!**

PLAN YOUR VISIT 40

Westonbirt Arboretum
Tetbury, Gloucestershire, GL8 8QS
www.forestry.gov.uk/westonbirt

📞 01666 880 220

🕐 Daily (summer) 09.00-20.00
Daily (out of season) 09.00-17.00 or dusk
Sat-Sun opens at 08.00

££

I want to go here ☐

CENTRAL BRISTOL
OUTER BRISTOL
BATH
N. SOMERSET
AROUND
ACROSS
TOP FIVES

GO ON A CANOE SAFARI

...at Slimbridge Wildfowl and Wetlands Centre

We like feeding the ducks in the park, but we LOVE seeing all the different types of birds on a Slimbridge canoe safari. It's a *fowl* (not a *foul*) experience!

Slimbridge is a special conservation park containing birds from all over the place. As well as being home to the world's largest collection of swans, geese and ducks, they are also regularly visited by wild birds who love the wetlands setting.

The canoe safaris are for up to three people, and give you a chance to spot animals you won't see from dry land. Look out for water voles, dragonflies, warblers and ducks. You'd be *quackers* not to visit!

Sticker Scores

DRAMATIC
DRAGONFLY

WONDERFUL
WARBLER

GREAT
GOOSE

DECENT
DUCK

BIRD-
BRAINED

CENTRAL BRISTOL

OUTER BRISTOL

BATH

N. SOMERSET

AROUND

ACROSS

TOP FIVES

Best Of The Rest

🔑 Feed the ducks and geese using the special grain that Slimbridge sells in its shop.

🔑 Touch frogs, toads and newts at Toad Hall. There are regular talks where you get the chance to handle the amphibians.

🔑 See a family of otters at the Back from the Brink exhibit. Flo, Mo, Minnie and Ha Ha are most active at feeding time.

🔑 Climb the tall tower in the visitor centre for a great view of Slimbridge.

What do you call a cat that has swallowed a duck?

A duck-filled fatty-puss!

Fascinating Facts

★ **Male ducks are called drakes and female ducks are known as hens. A group of ducks can be called a flock, a paddling or a raft.**

★ Slimbridge is particularly famous for the beautiful Bewick's swans which migrate there for the winter from arctic Russia. During the winter Slimbridge puts up floodlights so that you can see them eating on the lake.

Top Tip

If you're brave enough you can feed ducks and geese from your hand. Put the grain in the middle of your palm and hold it out flat so they don't nip your fingers. Do be careful as they can sometimes get a bit rough!

PLAN YOUR VISIT 41

Wildfowl & Wetlands Trust

Slimbridge, Gloucestershire, GL2 7BT

www.wwt.org.uk/visit-us/slimbridge

📞 01453 891 900

🕐 Daily (summer) 09.30-17.30
Daily (out of season) 09.30-17.00

££

I want to go here ☐

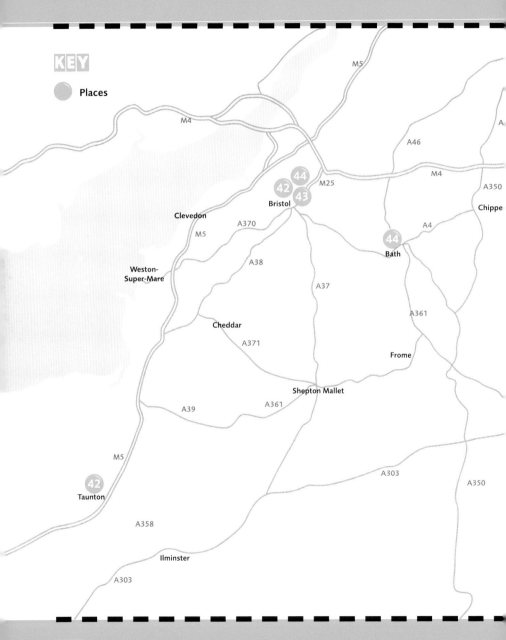

KEY

⬤ Places

M5

M4

A46

M4

A350

A

Chippe

M25

Bristol

44

42 43

Clevedon

A370

A4

M5

Bath

44

A38

Weston-
Super-Mare

A37

A361

Cheddar

A371

Frome

Shepton Mallet

A39

A361

M5

A303

A350

42

Taunton

A358

A303

Ilminster

A303

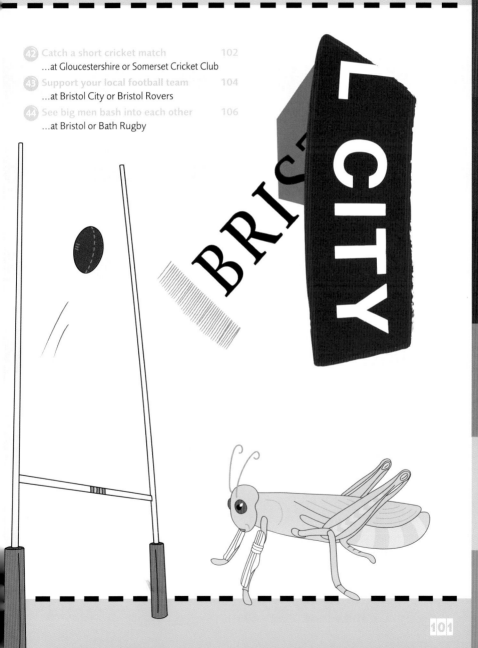

CENTRAL BRISTOL

OUTER BRISTOL

BATH

N. SOMERSET

AROUND

ACROSS

TOP FIVES

CATCH A SHORT CRICKET MATCH

...at Gloucestershire or Somerset Cricket Club

In the old days, all cricket games lasted for up to five days. Multi-day matches can be seriously exciting, but they can also drag on and on. And if it rains nobody plays anyway!

However, there is now also a newer form of cricket called Twenty20 where you have far more chance of a fun day out. Matches never last more than a few hours, and there's often music and other entertainment.

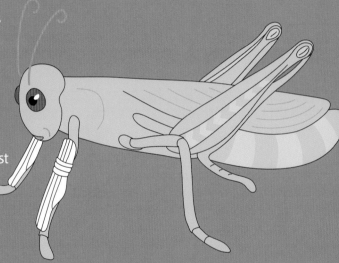

Sticker Scores

5 A BOWLER

4 BRILLIANT BATSMAN

3 FANTASTIC FIELDER

2 CRUMMY KEEPER

1 EBOLA

The two big Twenty20 teams in the region are Gloucestershire and Somerset. Both are good on their day – Somerset won the Twenty20 cup in 2005 and Gloucestershire were runners up in 2007. But most importantly, if you go to a match at least you know it will finish (unless it rains, that is)!

CENTRAL BRISTOL

OUTER BRISTOL

BATH

N. SOMERSET

AROUND

ACROSS

TOP FIVES

Top Tip

Take an umbrella to the game in case it rains. Not all parts of the grounds are covered and you wouldn't want to be stuck in a shower!

Why did the batsman have a dodgy stomach?

Because he'd got the runs!

Fascinating Facts

★ Many people think the greatest cricketer of all time was a man from Bristol called W.G. Grace. He played for 44 seasons, captained England and Gloucestershire, and once scored a whopping 344 runs in one innings. Oh, and he did all this while sporting a comically long beard and holding down a career as a doctor!

★ Cricket field positions often have bizarre names. For example, the person fielding at right angles to the wicket is the square leg. The person fielding in front and to the side of the batsman is the silly mid off. Presumably the name for someone standing directly in front of the batsman is silly idiot!

★ A cricket is a small insect with a flat body and thin legs. This means they're rubbish at playing cricket.

PLAN YOUR VISIT 42

Somerset County Cricket Club
The County Ground, Taunton, Somerset, TA1 1JT
www.somersetcricketclub.co.uk

☎ 0845 337 1875

Gloucestershire County Cricket Club
The County Ground, Nevil Road, Bristol, BS7 9EJ
www.gloscricket.co.uk

☎ 0117 910 8000

I want to go here ☐

...at Bristol City or Bristol Rovers

Watching the Premiership on the telly can be good fun – you get to see famous players who are household names. However, we think nothing beats seeing your local team play, whichever league they're in . . .

If you live in the Bristol area you have two talented and well-supported teams near you: Bristol City and Bristol Rovers. Both teams have histories stretching back to the 1800s, and both have spent recent years in the Championship, League One or League Two.

Mind you, if you are planning to watch a local match you'd better pick a team and stick with it. Rovers and City fans are big rivals, and so only a *soccer sucker* would try to support both!

Sticker Scores

5 WORLD CUP

4 CHAMPION'S LEAGUE

3 FA CUP

2 LEAGUE CUP

1 TEA CUP

CENTRAL BRISTOL
OUTER BRISTOL
BATH
N. SOMERSET
AROUND
ACROSS
TOP FIVES

Similar Spots

Why not check out one of the following clubs if you live nearby.

Bath City are a semi-professional side that have always played non-league football. www.bathcityfc.com

Cheltenham Town got to the last sixteen of the FA Cup in 2002. www.ctfc.com

Swindon Town had a spell in the Premier League in the early nineties. www.swindontownfc.co.uk

Yeovil Town have played in the Football League since 2003. www.ytfc.net

Fascinating Facts

⭐ **Bristol City are known as The Robins because that's the bird that used to appear on their club badge. Bristol Rovers are known as either The Pirates (because the city has a seafaring past) or The Gas (because their ground used to be near gasworks).**

⭐ Ian Holloway (a former Bristol Rovers player) is now a football manager known for saying strange things. For example, after winning promotion for Blackpool in 2010, he said: 'Every dog has its day, and today is woof day! Today I just want to bark!'. We just think he's *barking* mad!

Top Tip
Watching football is not always cheap, but Bristol Rovers has a family enclosure with good value tickets.

← Scrumpy the Robin, Bristol City's mascot

PLAN YOUR VISIT 43

Bristol City Football Club
Ashton Gate Stadium, Bristol, BS3 2EJ
www.bcfc.co.uk

📞 0117 963 0700

Bristol Rovers Football Club
The Memorial Stadium, Filton Avenue, Bristol, BS7 0BF
www.bristolrovers.co.uk

📞 0117 909 6648

I want to go here ☐

SEE BIG MEN BASH INTO EACH OTHER

...at Bristol or Bath Rugby

Footballers are well known for overreacting to even the smallest foul by rolling around on the floor. In rugby there's none of that. The players bash into each other with ferocious force . . . and you rarely see them complain about it!

Both Bristol and Bath have great rugby clubs that are usually in the top English league (the Premiership). That means that fans get to watch high quality matches and see famous international players.

Both clubs also have youth teams (Bath Youth Rugby and Bristol Youth Rugby) so if you're a real rugby nut then check the websites for how to get involved. And don't worry about being bished – the younger youth leagues play a tag version of the game!

Sticker Scores

5	4	3
SUPER SCRUM	TOP TACKLE	REASONABLE RUCK

2	1
LAME LINE OUT	SIN BIN

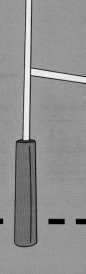

CENTRAL BRISTOL

OUTER BRISTOL

BATH

N. SOMERSET

AROUND

ACROSS

TOP FIVES

Similar Spots

Clifton has a well supported side that plays in the National Leagues. They also have a strong kids' set-up and organise teams for all ages from under sixes upwards.
www.cliftonrugby.co.uk

Top Tip

Bath offer a mini season ticket. This has nothing to do with small supporters! Instead it's a partial season ticket which allows you to attend several games for a discounted price.

Why couldn't the car play rugby?

It only had one boot!

Can you put me back now?

Fascinating Facts

★ Bath won the top league title in rugby an amazing six times in eight years from 1989 to 1996. Since then they've struggled with consistency but they're still one of the top teams in England.

★ Rugby was supposedly invented by a frustrated schoolboy named William Webb Ellis. Apparently he was playing football one day in 1823 when he decided that kicking the ball was boring, so instead he picked it up and ran with it!

★ A scrum in rugby involves eight people from each side (the pack) binding together in a big sporting cuddle. The players in the middle of the pack (the second rows) have to put their heads between the bums of the players at the front (the hooker and the props). *Ewww!*

PLAN YOUR VISIT 44

Bath Rugby
The Recreation Ground, Spring Gardens, Bath
www.bathrugby.com
www.bathyouthrugby.co.uk

📞 0844 448 1865

Bristol Rugby
The Memorial Stadium, Filton Avenue, Bristol, BS7 0AQ
www.bristolrugby.co.uk
www.bristolyouthrugby.co.uk

📞 0871 208 2234

££   I want to go here

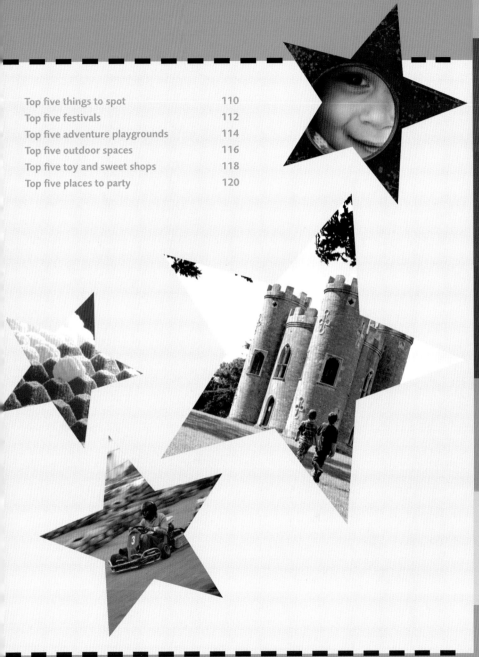

CENTRAL BRISTOL

OUTER BRISTOL

BATH

N. SOMERSET

AROUND

ACROSS

TOP FIVES

TOP FIVE

...things to spot

Whilst you're out and about exploring Bristol & Bath, make sure you keep an eye out for these local curiosities!

Iron Kerbs

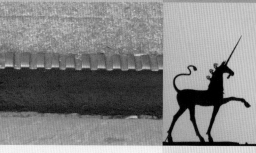

Roads are not normally made with metal, but in Bristol that's exactly what they used to do!

Serrated iron was put on the edges of pavements between the 1700s and the 1900s to keep cart wheels from damaging them. It was clearly effective as lots of the iron kerbing still exists! Look out for examples on Lower Park Row and Temple Street.

Unicorns

It's not just people who have coats of arms – cities can do too! Bristol's coat of arms contains two unicorns, and you ca see them in several places around the cit

Bristol's most famous unicorns are on top of the council house, by College Green. They're four metre tall and gold coloured! Yo also see unicorns on brid and public buildings arou the city – and also on the ss *Great Britain* (see p12).

CENTRAL BRISTOL

OUTER BRISTOL

BATH

N. SOMERSET

AROUND

ACROSS

TOP FIVES

Bristol Nails

Bristol's nails are not the sort you'll nd bashed into wood r on the end of your ngers. Instead they re big, round, metal tumps outside the Corn Exchange.

/hen Bristol's business eople did deals in the old ays they would put money n top of these nails to now that everything was greed. You can still see and ouch the four nails today just don't leave any cash n them!

Bath Stone

Bath stone is unsurprisingly a sort of stone which comes from Bath. It is extracted from nearby quarries and gives the city a very distinctive look.

The city's stone has a pretty honey-yellow colour. As well as being popular in Bath, it's also commonly used to build churches in other parts of southern England. And because Bath stone is a type of limestone, you can sometimes spot small fossils in it!

Banksy

Bristol-born Banksy has made graffiti into an art form – his creations regularly sell for tens of thousands of pounds!

Lots of graffiti is considered an eyesore, but if Banksy stencils something on your house it can dramatically increase its value. He now sprays all over the world, but because he's from Bristol many of his best works are here. Check out www.bristol-street-art.co.uk to see where he's left his mark.

TOP FIVE

...festivals

Everyone likes a good festival, and Bristol & Bath have some of the finest around. Here are five we particularly like.

I WENT TO:

- [ ] Bristol Balloon Fiesta
- [ ] Kite Festival
- [ ] Bath Festival of Children's Literature
- [ ] Bristol Harbour Festival
- [ ] Bristol Food Festivals

Bristol Balloon Fiesta

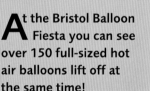

At the Bristol Balloon Fiesta you can see over 150 full-sized hot air balloons lift off at the same time!

The fiesta attracts half a million people to Ashton Court (see p43) over four days in August. There are mass lift-offs at 06.00 and 18.00, and a whole load of other entertainments besides. Look out for funny-shaped balloons – we've seen ones that look like a car, a chicken, a house and even a Scottish bagpiper!

www.bristolballoonfiesta.co.uk

Kite Festival

Kites have traditionally been considered a sign of peace and prosperity.

We can't promise you money and happiness, bu we do know that if you go to the Bristol Kite Festival September you'll have a l fun! The best bit is watchi hundreds of brightly coloured kites of all shape and sizes flying together. how many different anima kites you can spot – we've seen lizards, teddy bears, octopuses and pandas!

www.kite-festival.org.

CENTRAL BRISTOL

OUTER BRISTOL

BATH

N. SOMERSET

AROUND

ACROSS

TOP FIVES

ath Festival f Children's iterature

Bristol Harbour Festival

Bristol Food Festivals

f you like books (and you're reading this ne, so we assume ou do!), the Bath estival of Children's terature is a great lace to go.

mous authors, illustrators, nd storytellers come to ath to give talks about eir work and launch new ooks. You can hear your vourite author speak, et them to sign books for ou, discover how to draw ustrations and learn how tell stories in special orkshop sessions!

Bristol Harbour Festival focuses on **ships and boats. People flock to the docks to see attractions such as old-style tall ships.**

In addition there's a whole load of other things to do including circus and theatre shows, juggling, acrobats, face-painting, arts and crafts, salsa and other dancing. The highlight is the Sunday night firework display, which takes place above the harbour. We're sure it'll float your boat!

Bristol has some great food festivals **where you can walk along and sample a range of snacks.**

The Wine and Food Fair has chef demonstrations where you can see professionals cooking. There's also a cookery school for kids where you can learn to cook. The Organic Food Festival on Bristol's harbourside focuses on things that have been produced using organic methods. It's like a cross between a posh lunch and a day out!

www.bristolwineandfoodfair. co.uk
www.organicfoodfestival. co.uk

ww.bathkidslitfest.co.uk

www.bristolharbourfestival. co.uk

...adventure playgrounds

Adventure playgrounds are like normal playgrounds, only bigger and better! Here are five of the best in the Bristol & Bath area.

Hengrove Play Park

Hengrove is a state-of-the-art play park, and it's completely free to use! Don't be put off by the fact that it's at the back of a car-park, it's one of the best playgrounds around.

The park contains a massive dome with a cool jungle experience suspended from it. You'll also find lots of things to scramble around, play on and run through. Each bit is different – there are sand, water and grass areas, and also a separate section for skateboarders, roller bladers and BMX riders.

Hengrove Play Park
Hengrove Way, Hengrove, Bristol, BS14 0HR

Royal Victoria Park

Victoria Park has an awesome adventure playgrou[nd] complete with slides, swings and a[n] obstacle course.

But that's not all - there's plenty of space to play in cycle around, plus a pitch and putt golf course! If yc feel like it, you can feed t ducks . . . and even yours when the ice-cream van's there! Also look out for Bath's botanical gardens which are next to the par

Royal Victoria Park
Marlborough Lane, Bath, BA

CENTRAL BRISTOL

OUTER BRISTOL

BATH

N. SOMERSET

AROUND

ACROSS

TOP FIVES

Blaise Castle Adventure Playground

Bowood Adventure Playground

Lockleaze Adventure Playground

The adventure playground has logs to scramble over, things to balance along, ropes to swing on and a sandpit!

However, there's more to Blaise than the playground. Take a ride on the mini-railway or check out the Castle's collection of old toys and costumes. We also particularly love the huge outdoor spaces where you can fly kites, splash in rivers, crawl into caves and even walk under a waterfall!

Bowood's playground is so good that we've included it in this book twice! We think their adventure playground is one of the best in the country.

Apart from the life-size pirate ship, you'll find a dramatic death slide, super swings, cool chutes, terrific trampolines and super sticks to scramble over. And that's all before we've told you about the other things you can do at the estate (see p86)!

This great adventure playground has a big wooden tower with a whole load of walkways and gangways leading off it as well as a super scary death slide.

There's also an elevated roundabout, and all the usual *swing-tastic* playground stuff. It's not as grand as Bowood, but with a death slide this good you're sure to have a killer time!

Blaise Castle
Henbury Road, Bristol, BS10 7QS

Bowood House
Derry Hill, Calne, Wiltshire, SN11 0LZ
www.bowood-house.co.uk

Lockleaze Adventure Playground
Romney Avenue, Lockleaze, Bristol, BS7 9SU

TOP FIVE

...outdoor spaces

It's fun to visit big attractions, but sometimes all you need is a big outdoor space and your imagination. Here are our favourites...

I WENT TO:

- [ ] Bath Maze
- [ ] Arnos Vale Cemetery
- [ ] Ashton Court
- [ ] The Downs
- [ ] St. Andrew's Park

Bath Maze

Bath Maze is made from flat stones, so you're unlikely to get lost! It's also set in lovely gardens where you can let off some steam once you've mastered the maze.

At the centre of the puzzle you'll find a mosaic of the Gorgon – a snake-haired lady from Greek mythology whose face was so ugly that if you saw it you'd turn to stone. So you might want to think twice before staring at it!

Bath Maze
Beazer Gardens, Bath, BA2 1EE

Arnos Vale Cemetery

Strolling around amongst dead bodies might seem li a strange suggestion but Arnos Vale Cemetery is a great place to take a walk.

It's over 170 years old, and more than 300,000 people are buried here! There are a lot of interesti gravestones you can look out for, including a forme footballer's grave and the Indian-style tomb of Raja Ram Mohan Roy. The cemetery is also home to lot of wildlife.

Arnos Vale Cemete
Bath Road, Bristol, BS4 3EW
www.arnosvale.org.uk

CENTRAL BRISTOL

OUTER BRISTOL

BATH

N. SOMERSET

AROUND

ACROSS

TOP FIVES

Ashton Court   The Downs   St. Andrew's Park

Ashton Court is a massive estate full of places to play, hills to roll down and spots for kite flying.

that wasn't enough there's so a deer park, a golf course (see p42), a café nd a visitor centre. Ashton ourt estate is also home o amazing events like the alloon fiesta and the kite estival (see p112). It'll put ou in a great e-*state* of ind!

Ashton Court
ong Ashton, BS41 9JN
ww.ashtoncourtestate.
o.uk

The Downs is a huge open space in the middle of Bristol. The area is flat, grassy and perfect for running around on!

Why not take a ball or a frisbee and set up a sporting event? Or alternatively, take a bike and ride out to Clifton Gorge for a view of the suspension bridge (see p10)! Finally, head to Bristol Botanic Gardens on the edge of the Downs to learn about the evolution of plants. It's *plant*-astic!

The Downs
Stoke Road, Bristol, BS9

St. Andrew's park is not the biggest, but it is one of our favourites.

There's a paddling pool and a play park, and there's always a really friendly atmosphere – for example you'll often see people playing music. It's also in a convenient location behind Gloucester Road, so you can combine some shopping with some park play and a picnic! You won't find better in the centre of Bristol!

St. Andrew's Park
Effingham Road, Bristol, BS6.

TOP FIVE

...toy and sweet shops

Surely nobody needs any persuading that it's handy to know good places to buy toys and sweets! Here are our favourites in the region.

Sweetie Pie

Revilo Toys

Everything this shop sells really is *sweet*! Mind you, they don't have much in the way of pies . . .

Super-friendly shop assistants help you choose between fizzy laces, chocolate mice, jelly sweets, bon bons, gobstoppers and sherbet dips . . . In fact, they have almost every type of sweet you can think of. It's perfect for people with a sweet tooth!

Sweetie Pie

Unit 9, The Clifton Arcade, Boyces Avenue, Clifton, BS8 4AA

www.sweetiepiesweets.co.uk

Plastic is cheap an plentiful, so who would think of makir toys from anything else? Revilo *wood*, that's who!

Revilo specialises in kids' s made from wood. They st all sorts of colourful toys a games such as mobiles, ca jigsaws, musical instrumer And because they're mad wood, they are smarter an longer lasting than most to We think you'd be *bark*-in mad not to visit!

Revilo Toys

5:15 Paintworks, Bath Road, I BS4 3EH

0117 972 3195

www.revilotoys.co.uk

I WENT TO:

- ☐ Sweetie Pie
- ☐ Revilo Toys
- ☐ Hawkin's Bazaar
- ☐ Bath Sweet Shoppe
- ☐ Toys R Us

CENTRAL BRISTOL

OUTER BRISTOL

BATH

N. SOMERSET

AROUND

ACROSS

TOP FIVES

Hawkin's Bazaar

Bath Sweet Shoppe

Toys R Us

Hawkin's shops are always stuffed full of gadgets, gifts, and unusual toys of all types. We particularly like them because of the shop's 'do touch' policy, which means you can try most things before you buy.

The chain was started in a placed called the Hawk Inn, so that's where the name comes from. We think some of their toys are so strange (in a good way) that they should call it Hawkin's Bizarre instead!

Hawkin's Bazaar

10 Stall Street, Bath BA1 1QH

Unit 24, The Mall, Broadmead, Bristol, BS1 3XB

www.hawkin.com

These days you can of course buy sweets in most newsagents, but the selection will rarely be as good as this place!

Bath Sweet Shoppe is a traditional sweet shop jam-packed with a terrific range of treats in jars. You can create your own pick 'n' mix from boiled sweets, jelly babies, sherbet lemons and many more. Look out for the regular special offers where they put the sweets back to their old-fashioned prices!

Bath Sweet Shoppe

8 North Parade Passage, Bath BA1 1NX

01225 428 040

www.bathsweetshoppe.com

Good toy shops don't have to be big, but if you want a wide range to choose from then Toys R Us have the biggest shops around!

Toys R Us branches are massive, aircraft-hangar-sized warehouses full of toys, games, bikes, computer stuff and outdoor equipment (but sadly no actual aeroplanes). They also have one of the best websites if you prefer to buy your toys online.

Toys R Us

Cribbs Causeway, Centaurus Road, Bristol, BS34 5TU

Brislington Retail Park, Brislington, BS4 5NG

www.toysrus.co.uk

TOP FIVE

...places to party

Many of the places in this book are great for celebrations and events. However, here are a few venues that we think are particularly good for a pleasing party.

I WENT TO:

- [ ] Jungle Rumble Adventure Golf
- [ ] Hollywood Bowl
- [ ] Laser Quest
- [ ] Flying Saucers Cafe
- [ ] The Raceway

Jungle Rumble Adventure Golf

Normal golf courses are probably not the best places to hold a party. But at Jungle Rumble the golf is as crazy as the surroundings!

The crazy course contains eighteen holes of great golf including tribal huts, Aztec sculptures, a dark forbidding swamp, a live volcano and plenty of other obstacles. Everyone gets a party bag and the birthday girl or boy can buy a personalised t-shirt for friends to draw all over.

Jungle Rumble Adventure Golf
Cabot Circus, Bristol, BS1 3BQ
www.junglerumble.co.uk

Hollywood Bo

Bowling's the sort of game that's b when you're with lot: of friends – so it's ide for a birthday party!

At the Hollywood Bowl yo can bowl first then settle down to pizza, burgers or pasta (but don't try to stuf your face with all of them! When you're done you'll a framed photo to remind you of the day. Trust us, you'll want a *pizza* the acti

Hollywood Bowl
The Venue, Cribbs Causeway
Merlin Road, Bristol, BS10 7T
www.hollywoodbowl.c

CENTRAL BRISTOL

OUTER BRISTOL

BATH

N. SOMERSET

AROUND

ACROSS

TOP FIVES

.aser Quest

Flying Saucers Cafe

The Raceway

Playing Laser Quest is a bit like being tuck inside a real-life omputer game!

veryone gets a laser gun nen you have to shoot at our friends' guns without etting your own zapped the process. And don't orry if you think this ounds a bit too aggressive unlike actual wars, at a aser Quest party everyone ets together for an iced rink half way through!

Normally flying saucers in a café would be a bad thing. However, in this case Flying Saucers is the name of an awesome pottery painting café!

You and your friends choose a blank plate, bowl, mug or statue to decorate. You then sit in the special party room and create your own masterpiece. Once it's ready, it is fired in a kiln for you to collect a week later. It's not magic, it's *saucer*-y!

We always enjoy a party starting with go-karting. And at the Raceway you can zoom around at speeds of up to 45 mph!

All parties start with a lesson so you learn how to race safely. Then you get in your car and whoosh around the track racing against your friends. However, do remember that there are height restrictions and children need to be at least ten years old to race.

aser Quest

ne Old Fire Station, Sliver Street, oadmead, Bristol, BS1 2PY

w.lqbristol.co.uk

Flying Saucers, The Painting Pottery Café

9 Byron Place, Bristol, BS8 1JT

0117 927 3666

The Raceway

Avonmouth Way, Avonmouth, Bristol, BS11 9YA

www.theraceway.co.uk

PARENTS' PAGE

Hello adult. If you've read this far, you'll know that the rest of *Bristol & Bath Unlocked* is for kids. However, we didn't want you to feel left out so we've created this page especially for adults. If you're a child, stop reading now. Honestly, this isn't for you – it's very boring. If we were you, we'd go to p92 and find out how to come face to face with a lion. In fact, we suggest you do anything but read this page. Seriously, stop! Have you gone now? Good.

So anyway, hello, adult.

Bristol & Bath Unlocked is for children who are visiting places with adults. Very few of our sites admit unaccompanied children. Since you're likely to be the one planning the trip, we've included site details, such as telephone numbers and opening hours, on each page. Bear in mind that most sites are closed for Christmas, that bank holiday opening hours can vary, and that last admission is usually earlier than the closing time. We've also specified if there are height or age restrictions. While we have tried hard to ensure all the details are accurate at the time of going to press, things change, so it's best to check before you go anywhere.

Next: the Internet. We've tried to make sure that all our websites are child-friendly, but all the same, we suggest you supervise any surfing. We take no responsibility for third-party content and we recommend you check a site first if you are at all unsure.

Now for some general tips:

- Quite a few venues run good workshops and activities during weekends and school holidays. These are sometimes free, but may require advance booking.
- Many of the activities can be combined into a single day out. Use the maps at the beginning of each section to work out what things are near each other.
- Some of the activities in our book could be dangerous without appropriate adult supervision. Children using this book should be accompanied at all times.
- Many of the free activities in *Bristol & Bath Unlocked* involve walks on public land or visits to locations which don't have opening hours. We recommend you only go to such places during daylight, and make sure you leave enough time for the trip.

Oh, and one other thing. None of the sites in this book pay to be included – we've chosen them simply because we think they provide a jolly good day out.

Right then, that's the practical stuff out of the way, and there's still a page to fill. So we've selected some facts about Bristol and Bath just for grown ups. We don't think they're as interesting as the facts in the rest of the book, but then being an adult you don't really like interesting facts do you now?

- The Academy of Urbanism awarded their European City of the Year award to Bristol in November 2009.

- Bristol developed in Saxon times at the point where the River Avon and the River Frome meet. A bridge was built here and the settlement became known as Brigstowe, meaning bridging point. In time the name became Bristol, as locals have a tendency to add the letter 'l' on to the end of words. We thinkl that's a slightly strangel thing to dol.

- Bristol is a city, a unitary authority area and a ceremonial county. It is also home to around 420,000 inhabitants, few of whom care about the difference between a city, a unitary authority area and a ceremonial county.

- Bristol and Bath were in the county of Avon from 1974 to 1996, when Avon was abolished. However, some people still insist on referring to Avon, even though it doesn't exist any more. Frankly we're a bit bored of county boundaries anyway.

- Bath was an important city for the Romans, who were delighted to discover a hot spring there (as in warm water – they didn't find a warm Slinky lying on the ground).

- Sir Thomas Gainsborough, the 18th century adult and painter of people with silly haircuts, used to live in Bath. We think his pictures are quite dull but as you're a grown up you probably like them.

- People living in the South West are more likely to live to the age of 75 than those living elsewhere in England and Wales.

- Bristol and Bath is an anagram of hold tartan bibs.

OK, that's your lot. Time to hand the book back to your child. Or, if you are a child who's read all of this, we hope you learned that reading stuff meant for adults isn't going to be much fun.

INDEX

Here's an index of all the places included in the book, arranged in alphabetical order

INDEX

Where can you . . .

CENTRAL BRISTOL

OUTER BRISTOL

BATH

N. SOMERSET

AROUND

ACROSS

TOP FIVES

BACK-OF-THE-BOOK QUIZ
Good Luck!

The answers to all the following questions can be found somewhere in *Bristol & Bath Unlocked*. Email a correct set of answers to us and you'll have a chance to win a signed and framed illustration of your choice from the book!

1 What colour are Camargue horses when they are born?

2 What is a lorikeet?

3 Why is Bristol City Football Club known as the Robins?

4 How did Sooty celebrate his 60th birthday?

5 Do children have more bones in their bodies than adults?

6 Each stone at Stonehenge is as heavy as
A. 135 nine year old children
B. 1,350 nine year old children
C. 13,500 nine year old children

7 Cheddar Man is
A. A sculpture of a man made out of cheese
B. A mythical monster
C. A 9,000 year old skeleton

8 Which is NOT an ingredient used to make glass?
A. Sea
B. Sand
C. Salt

9 Which of the following do many lipsticks contain?
A. Fish scales
B. Fish bones
C. Fish eyes

10 What species of animal were Roberto and Amy, who got married at Wookey Hole Caves in 2008?
A. Frog
B. Rabbit
C. Porcupine

Tie-breaker

In no more than 30 words, tell us what is your favourite place in the book and why.

Send your answers to **quiz@factfinderguides.co.uk**

Full terms and conditions are on our website.

Joshua Perry and Emily Kerr

Emily and Josh went to school together in Bristol and still spend quite a bit of time in the region. So in a way they've spent their whole lives researching this book. Josh is (still) a big fan of sliding down the rock near Clifton Suspension Bridge and Emily loves looking at old dinosaur bones and glowing rocks in the Bristol Museum.

Allison Curtis

Allison lives near Bath in a proper house (though she used to live in a canal boat). When she's not designing Unlocked Guides she enjoys cycling along the canal towpath near her home, or paddling down the river in a boat. When she was a child she used to have two pet ducks called Francis & Firkin. She remains a big fan of the animals and is planning to start a duck welfare campaign.

Katherine Hardy (Kardy)

Kardy used to want to run a carousel when she was a kid. Then she grew up and realised that this wasn't exactly a money spinner, so she became an illustrator instead. At the moment she divides her time between London and New York, which makes her by far the most glamorous of the Unlocked team. She is planning to ride the donkeys in Weston-super-Mare sometime soon, and wishes that she could use them for her morning commute.

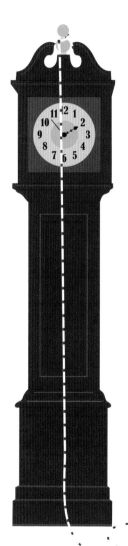

CREDITS

Authors: Emily Kerr, Joshua Perry
Series Editors: Joshua Perry, Emily Kerr
Design: Allison Curtis

Illustrations: Katherine Hardy
Maps: Allison Curtis, with reference to
OpenStreetMap – a free, editable map of the world

Thank yous ...

As always, everyone that helped us with the first three books. Here are some people who have provided some particularly awesome assistance.

Everyone at Bounce for being the best sales team in the world. Sandra Hedblad, Kate Rosser, Nicola Kalimeris, Anne McMeekin and Peter Matthews at the Museum of London for an incredible launch. Whatsonbristol and whatsonbath for many of the facts on the parents' page. James Crampton, Andy Cockburn and Matteo Rocchietta for being constantly generous with contacts and helpful with ideas. Harry Petrushkin for always being there. Anna Chomse and Steph Loader for general fantasticness. All the Halls for many days out in and around Bristol and Bath as a child, and for being a second family in London. Sophie and Thomas for saying exactly what they liked best on a fantastic day out. Anders Storbraten, Andrew Summers, Charlie Astor, David Yelland, Dea Birkett, Elizabeth Day, Emre Baran, Fiona Caulfield, Greg Marsh, Jonathan Knight, Keith Drew, Laura Burch, Louise Charlton, Maggie Bolger, Steve Watson, Titus Sharpe, Tom Burns, Tom Clifford, Tremayne Carew-Pole, Will Orr-Ewing for giving up their time to provide incredibly useful advice. As you might be able to guess, we like advice. Curtis for the bull joke. Jaime Fallon and Abby Hannan and the Cheese. Adam Thabo for his tree house. Carter Ballou Read for instructions on how to fish. Sarv Ghazanfar for the Persian rice. Anna Cory-Watson and the Hamptons charades team. Kimiyo Nakatsui for lending out her iron. Max Hardy for holding the fort. Terry Curtis, Nicole Holmes and Tony Kerr for the awesome additional proofing. Hannah Perry for fulfilling her company secretary duties by handing out pencils and bookmarks.

Photo Credits

11 Tony Kerr	65 Flickr, John Picken	112 ToysRUs
13 Tony Kerr	69 Flickr, Elliott Brown	113 Hawkin's Bazaar
15 courtenayphotography.co.uk	71 North Somerset Council	113 Flickr, Kirti Poddar
17 Neil Phillips	73 The Fleet Air Arm Museum	113 Flickr, Phil Campbell
19 Tony Kerr	75 Flickr, Yusuke Kawasaki	114 Bath Festivals
21 Bristol Zoo	77 Haynes Motor Museum	114 Flickr, Tom Roberts
23 Tony Kerr	79 The Helicopter Museum	115 Flickr, Antony Theobald
25 Flickr, Gary Bembridge	81 Wookey Hole Caves	115 Flickr, Karen
27 Flickr, Phil Crabbe	83 Brean Leisure Park	115 Flickr, Matt Buck
29 Adam Faraday	87 Bowood House	116 Tony Kerr
31 Bristol City Council	89 Flickr, Lawrie Cate	116 Simon Randolph
35 Concorde at Filton	91 Gloucester Waterways Museum	117 Tony Kerr
37 St Werburghs City Farm	93 www.longleat.co.uk	117 Flickr, Jared and Corin
39 Avon Valley Country Park	95 Berkeley Castle	117 Tony Kerr
41 Chris Bahn	97 Rob Cousins	118 Bath Tourism Plus
43 Tony Kerr	99 WWT Slimbridge Wetland Centre	118 National Trust
45 Horseworld	103 Flickr, Nick Townsend	119 Flickr, Thomas Guest
47 Waverley Excursions Ltd	105 Flickr, Chris Brown	119 Flickr, Ozan Kilic
49 Oakham Treasures	107 Martin Bennett photography	119 Flickr, Luis Argerich
51 Flickr, Shubert Ciencia	110 Tony Kerr	120 Jungle Rumble
55 Bath Aqua Glass	110 Tony Kerr	120 Flickr, Harsha KR
57 Bath & North East Somerset Council	111 Tony Kerr	121 Flickr, Peter Brooks
59 Andrew Desmond	111 Tony Kerr	121 Laserquest
61 Bath & North East Somerset Council	111 Flickr, Steve Cadman	121 Flickr, Josh Liba
63 The American Museum in Britain	112 Vanessa Clark	